Edinburgh, City of Funds

Investment management in Scotland's capital city

MARTIN FRANSMAN

Kokoro

Published by
Kokoro
41 Morningside Park
Edinburgh EH10 5EZ
United Kingdom

ISBN: 978-0-9557710-0-2

About the author

Martin Fransman is professor of economics and founder-director of the Institute for Japanese-European Technology Studies in the School of Business and Economics at the University of Edinburgh. He has published widely in the fields of innovation and competitiveness. His recent books include *Global Broadband Battles: Why the US and Europe Lag while Asia Leads* (Stanford University Press, 2006); *Telecoms in the Internet Age: From Boom to Bust to...?* (Oxford University Press, 2002); *Visions of Innovation: The Firm and Japan* (Oxford University Press, 1999); *Japan's Computer and Communications Industry: The Evolution of Industrial Giants and Global Competitiveness* (Oxford University Press, 1995); and *The Market and Beyond: Information Technology in Japan* (Cambridge University Press, 1990).

CONTENTS

PREFACE

This book is the first in a series titled *Entrepreneurship and Innovation*. The origins of this book go back to 1979 when I came to Edinburgh to take up a post in the Department of Economics at the University of Edinburgh. Shortly after arriving in the city I became interested in a puzzle. Edinburgh is a small European city with only approximately half a million people. It is not the capital of the United Kingdom nor one of its major commercial centres. Yet Edinburgh is the sixth biggest centre in Europe for fund management, following London, Paris, Zurich, Amsterdam and Frankfurt. These cities are either their country's capital or one of its major commercial centres. In 2007 £430 billion worth of investments were managed by specialist investment managers in Scotland, most of it in Edinburgh. Furthermore, Edinburgh is home to two of the United Kingdom's largest banks, the Royal Bank of Scotland and the Bank of Scotland. The Royal Bank is the sixth largest commercial bank in the world in terms of market capitalisation. Hence the puzzle: Why Edinburgh?

However, it was a chance event that allowed me to make some progress in tackling this question. In 2003 I was invited to Berlin to address a private meeting of members of *Institutional Investor*. My book, *Telecoms in the Internet Age*, which dealt with the telecoms boom and bust from 1996 to 2002, had just been published by Oxford University Press and I had been invited to give a lecture on this topic. At this meeting I had the good fortune to meet Richard Burns, former Joint Senior Partner at Baillie Gifford, Scotland's most successful independent investment manager, and one of the UK's too. In discussing the 'Edinburgh Puzzle' with Richard it soon became apparent that although a good deal of relevant research had been done there was little available that provided a robust answer. Richard and I agreed to pursue the matter on our return to Edinburgh.

The 'Edinburgh Puzzle' fitted in with two of my other interests; the one professional, the other personal. As a Schumpeterian evolutionary economist I had long been interested in the causes of long term economic development. I understood that although technology and innovation more generally were major drivers, institutions of various kinds also played a crucial role. One of these institutions is financial institutions. From my theoretical perspective they were best understood as a co-evolving phenomenon, changing in interaction with technical change and economic growth. But precisely how these general processes had worked in Scotland and, more to the point, how they produced Edinburgh as a city of funds and commercial banking was still unclear to me.

My personal interest was in biography. For some reason I have always been fascinated in seeing individuals, particularly interesting ones, situated in the changing historical circumstances of their time.

These two topics had made me interested in a third, namely entrepreneurship. As a colleague has observed, economic theory and the entrepreneur do not make good travelling companions. The reason is that the entrepreneur is a quirky character. He or she sees opportunities that others do not. Frequently the entrepreneur has a degree of motivation that others do not. Arguably, the would-be entrepreneur is also irrational since most of them fail. And, as Schumpeter has stressed, it is the collective actions of entrepreneurs that makes capitalism the incessantly restless system it is, perpetually causing disequilibrium by creating the new and destroying the old. Such quirkiness is difficult to reconcile with a conceptual framework based on the assumptions of rationality, optimisation and equilibrium.

In tackling the 'Edinburgh Puzzle' I would also be able to indulge these three interests. I soon came to the conclusion, influenced by my three interests, that although I had to understand the big picture in Scotland, a detailed study of one of the key players would provide important knowledge. Here the help of Richard Burns was invaluable as well as the information that he and his colleagues provided on Baillie Gifford.

My research into the big picture soon produced a significant insight. The answer to the Edinburgh fund management puzzle lies in a combination of entrepreneurship and innovation occurring within a specific set of broader economic circumstances, namely the accumulation of local pools of savings within the context of local economic growth. As this book shows, the contribution of four entrepreneurs was crucial: Robert Fleming; William Menzies; Carlyle Gifford; and, much later, Sandy Crombie. The first three were essentially diffusers of a key financial innovation that was started on 19 March 1868 in London, namely the investment trust. This book tells the story of how these events led ultimately to Edinburgh, city of funds.

In preparing this book I have been indebted to a number of people. First and foremost is Richard Burns who over the years has given a good deal of his time and knowledge to this enterprise. I am also grateful to him for writing the foreword which adds flesh to the story by providing a brief panorama of the other fund managers in Edinburgh whose stories have not been told in this book. Gavin Gemmell, Douglas McDougall and Max Ward, all leading senior partners at Baillie Gifford, also gave generously of their time and experience. Sandy Crombie, a key entrepreneur within Edinburgh's Standard Life who was involved in the establishment of Standard Life Investments, explained in a single interview the processes that led to the emergence of this important fund manager. The interpretations in this book, however, are my own.

At the University of Edinburgh I am grateful to Stuart Sayer, School of Business and Economics, who has encouraged this kind of work even though it detours somewhat from the conventional path followed in economics. Excellent research assistance, as always, has been provided by Ian Duff. Lynne McLaren has done her usual outstanding job in turning my sentences and tables into a publishable text. To all these people I am very grateful.

Entrepreneurship and Innovation

This book is the first of a series called *Entrepreneurship and Innovation*. This series aims at producing serious but accessible studies of entrepreneurs and their entrepreneurship.

Martin Fransman
Edinburgh
27 September 2007

FOREWORD

The financial sector in Edinburgh has traditionally been seen as honest, competent, stable and conservative. This was certainly the perceived wisdom when I started working in the city in the late 1960s. The scene was dominated, as has been the case for almost three centuries, by the two commercial banks, Bank of Scotland (the 'old bank', founded in 1695) and the Royal Bank of Scotland (the 'new bank', founded in 1727), though these were both small fish compared to their stature today. Next behind them in age and eminence were the life assurance companies. There were six of these, five operating as mutuals, with Standard Life and Scottish Widows standing out by virtue of their size and age (both were founded in the first quarter of the 19th century). The third element in the financial world consisted of the investment management businesses. Some of these, such as the Edinburgh Investment Trust and the Scottish Investment Trust, were continuing to carry on as free-standing self-managed investment trusts, which had first appeared in the city as Martin Fransman explains in 1873, but the majority operated as investment management businesses, the leading firms, at least as measured by size of assets, being Ivory & Sime, Baillie Gifford and Martin Currie. All these firms, although they were beginning to diversify their clientele, had as their core activity the management of investment trust companies.

Nothing that I have seen in the last 35 years has caused me to question the honesty and integrity of the financial institutions of the city. There have been numerous occasions in that time when individual businesses and firms have made serious mistakes and periods when the investment returns produced have been deeply disappointing to both managers and their clients or policy holders. Despite this, Edinburgh's reputation for competence has not been seriously called into question. Mistakes have certainly been made but these mistakes have been no worse than those made in other financial and investment centres. The conservative approach to business strategy has often been commented on. It has, of course, not been universal – both of the commercial banks tried to acquire National Westminster, which was substantially bigger than either, and the Royal was successful in a transaction which transformed it and did a huge amount to boost the mass and self-confidence of the whole Scottish financial sector. However, it would be true to say that, in general, Edinburgh's financial businesses have been rather cautious in relation to many of the new developments and opportunities of the last 30 years. For example, the 'Big Bang' of the mid-1980s, which led to an almost total reshaping of the landscape in London as stockbrokers, jobbers, bankers (both commercial and merchant) and some of the investment management businesses merged themselves into larger con-glomerated businesses, had virtually no impact in Edinburgh other than hastening the departure of Wood Mackenzie, a stock broking firm which had managed to join the big league of institutional stockbrokers but which was finding that it had increasingly to move its centre of gravity to London. Looking back with the benefit of 20 years of hindsight, it is arguable that not joining the 'Big Bang' game has proved to be the right decision; it is certainly the view of the partners of Baillie Gifford that their firm benefited greatly from maintaining its independence. It remains to be seen whether the reluctance of nearly (though not quite) all the established firms to get involved with the management of hedge funds will turn out to be a misjudgement of a great opportunity or a correct assessment of the difficulties which can arise when a hedge fund operation is placed alongside and within a traditional investment management business.

However, the one element of the traditional view which does not stand up to scrutiny, as clearly appears from Martin Fransman's book, is stability. In each of the three sub-sectors there has been considerable and continuing change, albeit sporadic, all through the 20th century. When I was a boy there were five note-issuing Scottish banks, the Bank itself, the Royal, the British Linen, the Clydesdale and the National Commercial. By 1971 this number had been reduced to three by the Royal merging with National Commercial and the Bank of Scotland buying British Linen from Barclays, which as a result acquired a 35% shareholding in the Bank. There then followed 30 years of calm, albeit interrupted by Standard Chartered's attempt to take over the

Royal Bank in 1981, before the transformation effected by the Royal's acquisition of NatWest in 2000 and the Bank's merger with the Halifax in 2002.

If change in the ownership and structure of the commercial banking sector is perhaps not so surprising, given that these were listed companies operating in a fairly transparent and high profile market, the changes in the life assurance sector in the last 20 years are very striking. In 1970, there were five independent life assurance companies based in Edinburgh, Standard Life, Scottish Widows, Scottish Equitable, Scottish Life and Scottish Provident. All were mutuals (Scottish Life having recently switched from being a proprietary company to a mutual to avoid the risk of policy holders' funds being asset-stripped by stock market raiders) and their long term viability as independent businesses seemed unquestionable. By the early 1990s, however, it was becoming apparent to the more far-sighted managements that the mutual life business model was not sustainable in the long term. Scottish Provident decided to exit the traditional life and pensions business and focus on the simple protection market; it eventually became part of Abbey National. Scottish Equitable sold itself to Aegon, Scottish Life to Royal London and Scottish Widows to Lloyds Bank. The Standard, as outlined in this book, having fought off a policy holder's attempt to force a demutualisation in 2000, eventually concluded that it would have to demutualise itself and floated in 2006. The consequence of these changes is that only three of the life companies, Standard, Scottish Widows and Scottish Equitable, are still carrying out investment operations in Edinburgh today.

Change in the fund management sector is perhaps less surprising than in the other two areas. The business entities are much smaller, the clients and customers fewer in number, the capital requirements relatively speaking minuscule and the scope therefore for start-ups and spin-offs from existing firms much greater. What we see from the time of William Menzies and the founding of SAINTS up to today is a picture of continual, though not continuous, change. A number of other investment trusts were founded in the last quarter of the 19th century, including the Scottish, floated in 1887 and still continuing in business as a stand-alone self-managed trust today, Investors Mortgage (now called Investors Capital and managed by Ivory & Sime since 1985), and the Edinburgh, whose management was moved from Edinburgh Fund Managers to Fidelity in London in 2002. The story of the Edinburgh Investment Trust in fact epitomises the theme of change. First established in 1889, it was for most of its life a self-managed trust. In 1985 it was decided that the team managing it should merge with the team at Belsize House in Dundee, which ran three other old established investment trusts, First Scottish American, Northern American and Dundee & London; a management company was formed called Dunedin Fund Managers. Not long after this merger was completed, British Linen Bank, by this time the merchant banking subsidiary of the Bank of Scotland, sold its investment management business to Dunedin in exchange for a controlling shareholding in the combined company. Then, in 1996 Dunedin was put up for sale by British Linen, the Bank of Scotland group having decided to exit the investment management business, and Dunedin was acquired by Edinburgh Fund Managers, which was itself a listed company whose aim was to grow both organically and by acquisition. Unfortunately for the shareholders of the Edinburgh Investment Trust investment performance had not been strong during much of this time and was showing no sign of improvement under the management of EFM. The Board therefore decided that the management contract should be terminated and in the 'beauty contest' which followed Fidelity, a Boston fund management company with a large operation in London, was successful in being awarded the contract, thus ending the Edinburgh Investment Trust's connection with the city. Or has it ended? In the last few months, Fidelity have hired two investment managers to work in its Edinburgh office, previously only used for sales …..

This is perhaps the extreme example of changes to an organisation but when the last 120 years are looked at as a whole it will be seen that the landscape of fund management has changed often, with the pace of change accelerating over the last 25 years. Both Ivory & Sime and Martin Currie were accounting firms which were in business as investment managers running investment trusts before the death of Queen Victoria and there were, as noted, several self-managed investment trusts, of which SAINTS was the longest established. Baillie and Gifford formed their partnership in 1907 and floated the company that would become

Scottish Mortgage in 1908. Other investment trusts were floated before the First World War and many more during the 1920s, a period of stock market boom, particularly in the United States. By the outbreak of the Second World War Carlyle Gifford, the dominant partner in his firm, was also clearly the outstanding figure on the Scottish investment scene. By the 1960s, however, Ivory & Sime, driven forward by the energetic ambition of Jimmy Gammell, was emerging as the leading, and certainly the most dynamic, firm and by the 1970s was vying with the investment operation of S.G. Warburg to be the largest manager of segregated pension fund assets in the UK. Meanwhile, the manager of SAINTS, Jack Shaw Stewart, had in 1970 organised the setting up of an investment management firm called Stewart Fund Managers to take on the management of SAINTS (which was itself a share-holder in the new management company) and other investment trusts or funds, if they could be floated or recruited as clients, in the same way as the old established management companies were managing investment trusts and other funds. A similar process at the American Trust produced Edinburgh Fund Managers, a firm which placed greater emphasis on unit trusts than its local competitors.

By 1980, Ivory & Sime was clearly the leading Edinburgh investment firm, while Baillie Gifford, as narrated by Martin Fransman, was in crisis. However, this situation did not last for long. Ivory & Sime had abandoned its partnership structure in the 1970s, largely for tax mitigation reasons, and Jimmy Gammell had deliberately fostered competition between the members of the next generation of (former) partners. This produced considerable internal turmoil after he retired and led in due course to a series of departures of senior people. Notable among these were Stewart Newton, who went to London and set up Newton Investment Management, which proved hugely successful over the next 20 years, and Walter Scott, who took many of Ivory & Sime's large American pension funds with him to his new firm, Walter Scott & Partners. Ian Rushbrook set up Personal Assets, an idiosyncratic but successful reversion to the self-managed investment trust with its own manager, and, symbolically, James and Ian Ivory, great-grandsons of one of the founding partners of Ivory & Sime, joined Stewart Fund Managers, which was renamed Stewart Ivory.

Aberforth Partners and Artemis are two other firms which were set up by former Ivory & Sime people and which have grown into significant and well regarded businesses. Ivory & Sime itself, after a rather unhappy period as a listed company, was used as a vehicle by the Friends Provident life assurance company to valorise its own investment management operations; Ivory & Sime plc issued a controlling interest in its share capital to Friends, which passed the contract for managing its funds, and its investment personnel to the new company, Friends Ivory & Sime. This was later renamed Isis and has since merged with Foreign & Colonial Asset Management. A smallish investment management operation and office in George Street (albeit with the finest view in Edinburgh) is all that now remains of what 30 years ago looked likely to become one of the UK's most successful investment firms. The magnificent Adam building at One Charlotte Square, the Edinburgh financial world's best address, is now occupied by Walter Scott & Partners (and the firm, though not the building, is owned by an American bank).

However, the story is not all one of change and passing glory. As well as Artemis and Aberforth, other new firms have emerged, such as Scottish Value Managers, whose Colin McLean has been one of the few Scottish based investors to engage seriously in hedge funds, and Edinburgh Partners, led by Sandy Nairn, which has quickly built up a sizeable pension fund business from modest beginnings with a small investment trust and some Dublin registered OEICs. As well as these 'native' businesses, two very large American fund management businesses, Templeton and Blackrock, have set up significant investment operations in Edinburgh in the last 15 years.

We shall have to wait and see whether these new businesses will be able, or indeed choose, to grow to rival the scale of their longer-established competitors. What does seem likely, however, is that the change which has always occurred but has undoubtedly become faster and more pervasive in the last 20 years will continue. This should give good scope for entrepreneurial individuals of the type described in this book to exercise their talents. It may mean that conservatism of strategy becomes a less marked feature of the Edinburgh financial sector in the years to come. It is to be hoped that the tradition of honesty and competence that is our inheritance from the past is not compromised in an ever-more changing and entrepreneurial environment.

Richard Burns
Former Joint Senior Partner, Baillie Gifford
Edinburgh
September 2007

INTRODUCTION

EDINBURGH, CITY OF FUNDS

Edinburgh is a city of fun. As most Europeans know, it is a city of culture, hosting one of Europe's most famous festivals. Edinburgh is also an important city historically, but not in the way of many other European cities that have played significant national or regional roles. As home to path-making thinkers such as David Hume and Adam Smith in the 18th century, Edinburgh can justifiably claim to have helped shape the Enlightenment which changed fundamentally the way in which people understand themselves, their societies and economies.

But Edinburgh is also a city of funds. This is perhaps not as well known popularly as Edinburgh's other characteristics. Many will be surprised to learn that in 2007, £430 billion worth of investments – including the funds of some of the world's largest pension and insurance funds – were managed by specialist investment managers in Scotland, most of it in Edinburgh. Indeed, Edinburgh is the sixth largest European city in terms of investment funds managed, coming after London, Paris, Zurich, Amsterdam and Frankfurt. Yet Edinburgh has a population only of around half a million, making it one of Europe's smaller distinguished cities.

How did Edinburgh become a city of funds? This is the main question dealt with in this book.

The story that answers this question, as will be shown in detail, is essentially one of economic growth, entrepreneurship and innovation. This story is told here through the eyes of some of the key people who played a leading role in initiating and growing the investment management sector in Scotland and Edinburgh.

FOUR INVESTMENT MANAGEMENT ENTREPRENEURS

Attention is focused in this book on four of these entrepreneurs. In historical order they are Robert Fleming, William Menzies, Carlyle Gifford and Sandy Crombie.

The initiatives of Fleming and Menzies are situated within the broader context of the co-evolution of technology, the growth of firms and industries and the related development of financial institutions in 18th and 19th century Scotland. It was this context that provided the opportunities that were seen and seized by Fleming and Menzies.

More specifically, the context of economic growth in Scotland over this period created the savings pools that these men drew upon in creating their entrepreneurial vehicles. In Fleming's case it was the textile industry magnates in the Dundee area – such as the Baxters and the Coxes – whose substantial incomes provided the savings that generated the fuel. However, Menzies, a lawyer, relied largely on the wealthy populace of Edinburgh – a combination of professionals, business people and local landowners.

However, this story also emphasises that it was a key innovation that lay at the heart of their activities, an innovation that was made in 1868 in London, precisely five years before first Fleming and then Menzies started in Scotland. Indeed, it is accurate to see Fleming and Menzies as entrepreneurial diffusers of this key innovation.

What was this innovation? The answer is the investment trust.

THE INNOVATION: THE INVESTMENT TRUST

The investment trust was a financial innovation that was launched on 19 March 1868. The concept behind this innovation was simple enough; by pooling resources, smaller savers, led by experienced professionals, would be able to do collectively what they could not do individually, namely earn a premium risk-adjusted rate of return on their savings over and above that available on alternative domestic financial assets such as consols and bank deposits.

In many respects the commercial bank itself was a similar innovation. The commercial bank was also an institution that could do collectively for savers and depositors what they could not do for themselves, namely increase the risk-adjusted return on their savings and deposits.

As an institution, the commercial bank was able to develop special competencies, embodied in banking practices and routines, to evaluate the returns that could be made from loans to various kinds of borrowers, including assessing the risks involved and monitoring the performance of the loan. Furthermore, by lending to large numbers of borrowers, commercial banks were able to reduce risk by spreading it. Although commercial banking began historically as a diversification undertaken by existing businesses – the goldsmiths being an example – the competencies and scale needed soon resulted in the emergence of commercial banks as a specialised institution.

Economists such as the Nobel Prize winner, Joseph Stiglitz, have pointed out that these kinds of financial institutions have evolved as a solution to problems of information asymmetry. There is an essential asymmetry between borrower and lender. For example, the lender may lack information regarding the borrower's intentions, the uses to which the loan will be put, the returns to these uses and the risks involved. Furthermore, it may be expensive to obtain this information or the information may simply not be available. Under these circumstances, Stiglitz notes, markets and prices cannot provide a sufficient solution. For instance, auction markets cannot be used to allocate scarce loans to would-be borrowers based on the highest price offered. Accordingly, financial institutions such as the commercial bank and investment trust have evolved that deal internally with the problem through practices that ameliorate as far as possible the difficulties arising from asymmetric information.[1]

The first investment trust which began on 19 March 1868 was the Foreign & Colonial Government Trust. One dimension of the asymmetric information problem – namely the lack of information on the part of potential investors in the trust regarding the competencies, intentions and reliability of the founders – was

---

[1]   See Greenwald, B. and Stiglitz, J.E. 1992. 'Information, Finance and Markets: The architecture of allocative mechanisms'. In V. Zamagni (ed), *Finance and the Enterprise*. London: Academic Press, pp.11-36.

resolved by the distinguished background of the trust's three founders, Philip Rose, Samuel Laing and James Thompson Mackenzie.

All were extremely well-known and well-connected and had made substantial sums of money in the railways boom. Furthermore, they had all been involved for five years already in forming and managing the General Credit & Finance Company (GCFC), one of the first major finance companies to be established after the passage of the 1862 Companies Act. Indeed, it has been suggested that the kernel innovative idea behind the investment trust was already present in the GCFC. The first Chairman of Foreign & Colonial was Lord Westbury, who had been Solicitor-General, Attorney-General and Lord Chancellor.

An important additional attraction offered by the Foreign & Colonial Government Trust was the higher returns that came from investments in overseas markets where market rates of return were significantly greater than in the UK. Wealthy investors had sufficient resources to create substantial portfolios that would allow them to take advantage of the higher returns while lowering risks by spreading them. Investment trusts, by pooling the funds of smaller savers, would offer similar advantages for those less well-off. The objective was succinctly explained in the Foreign & Colonial Government Trust's first prospectus: "To provide the investor of moderate means the same advantage as the large capitalist in diminishing risk in Foreign & Colonial stocks by spreading the investment over a number of stocks".[2] While in 1868 consols yielded 3.3%, Foreign & Colonial promised an expected yield of 7%.[3]

With the important benefits provided by this financial innovation, namely the investment trust, it is little wonder that it diffused rapidly to other parts of Britain, including Scotland. Under the contextual conditions examined in detail in this book Robert Fleming became the first financial entrepreneur in Scotland to diffuse this innovation, establishing his investment trust in Dundee on 1 February 1873, five years after Foreign & Colonial.

---

[2]   Newlands, J. 1997. *Put Not Your Trust in Money: A history of the investment trust industry from 1868 to the present day.* London: Chappin Kavanagh, 15.
[3]   ibid, pp.15 and 13.

Barely two months later, on 29 March 1873, Menzies founded his trust in Edinburgh.

In narrating the story of the evolution of the investment management sector in Scotland and Edinburgh a second story emerges. This is the story of the triumph of commercial banking in Edinburgh. Most triumphant has been Scotland's second bank (in historical order), the Royal Bank of Scotland, now the sixth largest commercial bank in the world by market capitalisation.

THE TRIUMPH OF EDINBURGH'S COMMERCIAL BANKS

This second story raises an important puzzle. Why did Edinburgh become the main Scottish centre for commercial banking rather than Glasgow? This question is all the more puzzling when the astounding success of the Glasgow area during the second industrial revolution – the revolution of steam and railways – is recollected. Glasgow's global role at this time was remarkable:

"By 1913, Glasgow and its satellite towns in the surrounding region of intensive industrialization produced one-half of British marine-engine horsepower, one-third of the railway locomotives and rolling stock, one-third of the shipping tonnage and about a fifth of the steel. On the eve of the First World War the Clyde not only built one-third of British output but almost a fifth of the world's tonnage, a record that was greater at the time by a considerable margin than all the German yards combined. At the heart of the heavy industrial complex with its world-wide markets was the huge range of engineering specialisms in engines, pumps, hydraulic equipment, railway rolling stock and a host of other products".

The Glasgow area dominated Europe's locomotive production:

"Three of the four greatest firms building locomotives were in Glasgow; in 1903 they came together to form the North British Locomotive Works, 'the Titan of its trade' with a capacity to produce no fewer than 800 locomotives every year. This made the city the biggest locomotive-manufacturing centre in Europe, with engines being produced in large numbers for the Empire, South America and continental countries".[4]

In strong contrast, Edinburgh, primarily a professional regional capital as documented in this book, boasted few companies the size of Glasgow's. So why did Edinburgh, rather than Glasgow, become Scotland's dominant centre for commercial banking?

The succinct answer to this question – that emerged only gradually over many years – can be given in one phrase: path-dependence. Essentially, Edinburgh's two main commercial banks – the Bank of Scotland, which was founded in 1695, and the Royal Bank of Scotland, started in 1727 – were established and had consolidated their business position in Edinburgh before the industrial revolution transformed the west of Scotland around Glasgow. As this revolution generated the demand for bank financing so the Edinburgh banks were best-placed to deliver it. The later-comers – newer and smaller banks established later in Glasgow – proved in the longer run unable to compete.

However, this raises the question of whether there is a link between the two stories. It is not difficult to imagine a link. It could be hypothesised, for example, that commercial banking would lead to the accumulation of funds, the management of which would lead to the emergence of a specialised investment management function within these commercial banks that, given their scale and financial connections, would come to dominate the investment management sector. But in fact, as this book shows, this was not to occur to a significant extent, although it did happen to some degree. The main investment managers in Scotland today are not the major commercial banks but rather specialist managers, some of whom are independent and some part of larger insurance

---

[4]   Devine (1999), pp.249-50.

groupings. The two stories, therefore, although having some connections, are largely independent.

BAILLIE GIFFORD

Most of this book is devoted to a detailed examination of the evolution of Scotland's most successful independent investment manager (and one of the UK's too), namely Baillie Gifford. By 2008 Baillie Gifford managed over £50 billion from Edinburgh. Its customers included five of the seven largest pension funds in the US and the firm – significantly, a private partnership – also has large businesses in Japan and Australia and has in the last two years acquired clients in other countries in the Far and Middle East, emphasising its successful globalisation.

Baillie Gifford was established in 1907 in Edinburgh by Colonel Augustus Baillie and his young partner, a newly-qualified lawyer by the name of Carlyle Gifford. Gifford would later go on to play a key role in Britain's Second World War effort, representing the Bank of England in liquidating British-owned assets in the US in order to help finance the war. [Less successfully, he would also enter into a partnership with John Maynard Keynes, establishing an investment company that later failed.]

At first, Gifford played the same kind of entrepreneurial role as that of Fleming and Menzies, diffusing the same innovation, namely the investment trust. Details are provided in Chapter 3 of the saving pools that Baillie Gifford tapped in the Edinburgh area.

The story of Baillie Gifford, however, unlike that of Fleming and Menzies, is pursued to the present time, showing in detail how the firm was able to grow its competencies, accumulating the ability to manage larger and larger quantities of investment funds and extending its activities on a global scale.

Of particular interest are the crises that the firm went through – which stimulated further innovations and initiatives – and its special form of ownership and governance, the private partnership, which Baillie Gifford believes is still a key source of its distinctive competitive advantage. Most importantly, this study of Baillie Gifford reveals how it is possible for an investment manager in

Edinburgh – far from the main centres of economic growth in the global economy – to do a fine job spotting investment opportunities in these far-flung parts of the world and turning them into good rates of return.

STANDARD LIFE INVESTMENTS

The last part of this book examines a variation of the Edinburgh investment management story, one focusing not on commercial banks but on insurance companies, another key successful financial institution based in Edinburgh. The firm in question is Standard Life Investments (SLI).

Standard Life began as an Edinburgh life insurance company in 1825. It started as a diversification by a fire insurance company that had been established four years earlier. Here the story is similar to the hypothesis made above that was rejected in the case of the Scottish commercial banks.

To put the story in a nutshell, over time Standard Life developed investment management competencies by investing funds that had been accumulated through the receipt of life insurance premiums. As these competencies grew over time, the entrepreneurial decision was made in 1998 to spin-off the investment management function in a new subsidiary, Standard Life Investments (SLI). SLI would not only manage internally generated funds supplied by the mother company (Standard Life), but also compete with firms like Baillie Gifford in the external market for investment management. The 'intrapreneur' who pioneered this entrepreneurial initiative, as is detailed in this book, was Sandy Crombie who implemented the decision that he and Scott Bell had taken to separate the company. SLI, therefore, provides an example of a different kind of entrepreneurship from that represented by Fleming, Menzies and Gifford, an entrepreneurship occurring within a large, established firm but an entrepreneurship nonetheless.[5]

---

[5] It is of relevance to note in this connection that Joseph Schumpeter, who more than anyone else analysed the role of entrepreneurship in the dynamics of change in capitalist economies, acknowledged the importance of

CONCLUSION

This, in summary, is the story of how Edinburgh became a city of funds. In the concluding chapter a more conceptual account is provided of the explanation of Edinburgh's success in investment management. Clearly, it is not the full story. There are important gaps that need to be filled with details of the contributions made by many others associated with investment management in Edinburgh and their firms. But it is a story that contains many of the essential ingredients that, collectively, explain why and how Edinburgh became the city of funds that it is today.

---

entrepreneurship in large, existing companies even though he also stressed the role of the individual entrepreneur.

CHAPTER

2

HOW DID EDINBURGH BECOME BRITAIN'S SECOND CITY FOR INVESTMENT MANAGEMENT?

THE EMERGENCE OF EDINBURGH AS A FINANCIAL CENTRE

The Bank of Scotland

By the early 1700s, well before the onset of the Industrial Revolution which began around 1770, Edinburgh was already a growing financial centre. The Bank of Scotland had been established in 1695, one year after the Bank of England. It was a product of a coalition of interests involving Scottish merchants (in Edinburgh and, more importantly, in London) with "...the active support of the Scottish political establishment of the day..."[1] and with further support from landowners.[2]

The main factor motivating the bank's establishment was the higher cost of finance being paid by Scottish merchants compared to their English counterparts. Cameron (1995) suggests three reasons for wanting to establish a bank with a strong London presence:

"By the 1690s the settlement of bills of exchange, the principal method of financing international trade, was already concentrated in London. Scots traders, as aliens

---

[1]   Cameron, A. 1995. *Bank of Scotland, 1695-1995*. Edinburgh: Mainstream Publishing, p.13.

[2]   ibid, p.18. The landlords, however, were the weakest partners in the coalition and there were soon complaints that their interests were not being adequately met.

[before the union of the Scottish and English parliaments in 1707], were at a distinct disadvantage in this market. They were offered less favourable rates than the English and often had to use rival English traders as intermediaries in negotiations".[3]

There was, however, a second reason:

"A second and more serious reason was that ever since the collapse of the Scottish Mint in 1681 the Scots coinage had been one of the more unreliable European currencies... Paper currency, in the shape of bills of exchange expressed in pounds sterling, seemed to offer precisely what the Scots coinage could not.

"A third element was the need for credit facilities within Scotland".[4]

The hope was that the Bank of Scotland would be able to reduce these costs. It was Thomas Deans, "...himself a banker and general entrepreneur, who, together with other Scots merchants in London, conceived the idea of a Scottish bank".[5] However, it was an Englishman, John Holland, who had worked for the East India Company, to whom they eventually turned to give effect to their plans for the establishment of a bank.

The Bank of Scotland was established by an Act of Parliament. It was "...the first example in Europe of a joint-stock bank being founded by private persons to make a trade of banking, wholly dependent upon the capital raised from its stockholders".[6] Its shareholders – or "Adventurers", as they are described in the Act – reflected the founding coalition. Of the total of 172 Adventurers, 136 lived in Scotland and 36 in London. In Scotland

---

[3] ibid, p.14.
[4] ibid, pp.16-7.
[5] Checkland, S.G. 1975. *Scottish Banking: A History, 1695-1973*. Glasgow: Collins, pp.17-8.
[6] Cameron (1995), p.14.

they included 24 nobles, 39 landed proprietors, 41 merchants, 14 lawyers and judges, and 7 women subscribing in their own right.[7]

The Royal Bank of Scotland

The Bank of Scotland was given monopoly rights for a period of 21 years that ended in 1716. By this time the Bank of Scotland had become rather isolated politically. It was regarded as a supporter of the Stuart cause and, equally important, as having failed to support the needs of Scottish trade and commerce.[8] Furthermore, a powerful Whig alliance had emerged in Edinburgh around Lord Islay (later the third Duke of Argyll), that included George Drummond, the Lord Provost of Edinburgh. When Robert Walpole became Whig Prime Minister after the collapse of the South Sea Bubble, "...it was necessary for him to be able to control the political allegiance of Scotland. To this end he relied upon the Scottish Whigs under Argyll. In return, it was necessary to do something for Scotland".[9]

The Whigs supported the idea of a second public bank in Scotland in the hope that it would enhance the development of the country. This led to the granting of a charter for the new Royal Bank of Scotland on 31 May, 1727. According to Checkland (1975): "The founding of the Royal Bank may be seen, not unfairly, as part of Walpole's system of political control in Scotland".[10]

In strong contrast to the Bank of Scotland, the Royal Bank "...was not a merchants' bank".[11] There were no merchants on the Royal Bank's directorate until 1730: "Instead, the directorate was composed of landlords, lawyers (no less than ten out of twenty...were judges) and men of good connections.... But the Bank's Cashier and his staff quickly became professionals".[12] The Royal Bank, however, soon developed a much stronger London

---

[7] ibid, p.21.
[8] Checkland (1975), p.58.
[9] ibid, p.57.
[10] ibid, p.59
[11] ibid, p.62.
[12] ibid, p.62.

connection than the 'Old Bank' (i.e. the Bank of Scotland) and used it to its advantage.[13]

Glasgow, Tobacco and the Banks

By 1745 the commercial centre of gravity of Scotland had shifted to the west of the country. Although traders and merchants in the west had been involved in trans-Atlantic trade since the 17th century (with official approval from the English since the Union of the Parliaments in 1707), it was from the mid-1700s that this became substantial. Particularly important was the tobacco trade,[14] largely with Virginia, which ushered in a golden age after about 1740.[15] By 1765, Scots were responsible for 40% of the total UK tobacco trade.[16] According to Devine (2003): "The tobacco trade was Scotland's first global empire. Because of it, Glasgow became a player on the world commercial stage by the 1770s".[17]

The tobacco trade was highly concentrated, dominated by a small number of families and trade associations. In 1742, for example, "...over two-thirds of the tobacco landed was shipped by just four family syndicates, the Dunlops, Bogles, Oswalds and McCalls. The bulk of the remaining cargoes was landed by a further six associations of merchants".[18] However, by 1745 the tobacco lords, or 'Virginian dons' as they were called, were "...dependent upon Edinburgh for its banking facilities. Neither of the public banks [i.e. the Bank of Scotland and the Royal Bank] had a Glasgow branch. But both had a syndicate of powerful associates there, composed of leading men in the tobacco trade".[19]

---

[13] ibid, pp.63-4.

[14] The sugar trade, from sugar plantations in the Caribbean, was also important but not as significant for Scotland as the tobacco trade. See Devine, T.M. 2003. *Scotland's Empire, 1600-1815*. London: Allen Lane, pp.221-9.

[15] ibid, p.85.

[16] ibid, p.320. Amongst the reasons for Scottish prominence in the tobacco trade was the shorter trade route between Scotland and America and the well-developed trading relationship between Scotland and Europe (particularly France) which assisted the re-export of tobacco imported from America.

[17] ibid, p.71.

[18] ibid, p.88.

[19] Checkland (1975), p.88.

Nevertheless, the 'tobacco men' had the power to try and change this in order to increase the benefit that they themselves derived from their trade. As Checkland (1975) notes, they were "…indeed a powerful civic and commercial oligarchy, of a kind which must emerge when the trade of a rising city is specialised and large-scale as in Venice, Amsterdam and elsewhere: in Glasgow the tobacco lords had control of the magistracy and the Merchants House (traders' guilds)".[20]

They therefore were behind the establishment of several Glasgow-based banks that proceeded to challenge the dominance of the Edinburgh public banks. These included the Ship Bank, established in 1749 (which originally was established under the aegis of the Bank of Scotland but then asserted its independence), and the Thistle Bank set up in 1761. The formation of the Ship Bank (and about the same time, the Glasgow Arms Bank by a larger group of Glasgow merchants not dominated by the tobacco barons) led to the so-called third bank war from 1749-61 as the Edinburgh public banks retaliated.[21]

Edinburgh's Financial Dominance

However, none of these Glasgow-based banks were able to mount a serious challenge to Edinburgh's two public banks supported by a number of private banks. In explaining this Checkland (1975) gives as reasons the fear of another bank war, the indifference of the tobacco lords to a national challenge in banking and the reluctance or inability to merge to constitute a bank of larger size.[22] Edinburgh, however, having seen off the Glasgow challenge for the time being, was able to consolidate its considerable advantages:

> "Edinburgh, …though no longer a political capital, did enjoy real advantages. It was still the centre for the nobility and landed men, and for the law courts and the church. In finance, the Bank of Scotland and the Royal

---

[20] ibid, pp.106-7.
[21] ibid, pp.97-108. See also Devine (2003), pp.84-5 (though Devine gives 1752 as the founding date for the Ship Bank c.f. Checkland (1975), pp.97-8).
[22] Checkland (1975), p.107.

Bank had established themselves in the centre of Scottish life, sustained by their associates, the Edinburgh private banks. It was upon Edinburgh that landed savings converged, as did landed borrowings, still the largest elements in the nation's credit transactions. Moreover, the public banks had learned that the interests of both lay in mutual respect and mutual aid against interlopers, operating through a pact of amity. The Glasgow banks were never to achieve this solidarity".[23]

Despite the dominance of Edinburgh, however, thanks largely to strong competition in a multi-bank system, Scotland was able to develop a highly efficient banking system. Indeed, "...by 1772 the Scottish banking system was the most developed in Europe".[24]

The Edinburgh banks were able to further consolidate their position by opening branches in Glasgow. In 1783, the Royal Bank opened its Glasgow branch, which subsequently became the dominant bank in Glasgow, and the Bank of Scotland followed suit in 1787.[25]

TECHNICAL CHANGE, ECONOMIC GROWTH AND FINANCIAL DEVELOPMENT

A simplified model of the relationship between technical change, economic growth and financial development is useful at this stage in order to assist the analysis of the development of financial institutions in Scotland from the time of the Industrial Revolution and the contextualisation of the origins of Baillie Gifford and Standard Life Investments.

According to this model, radical technical change (sometimes accompanied by radical scientific change) creates new

---

[23] ibid, p.108.

[24] ibid, p.92.

[25] Munn, C.W. 1994. 'The Emergence of Edinburgh as a Financial Centre'. In A.J.G. Cummings and T.M. Devine (eds), *Industry, Business and Society in Scotland since 1700:Essays presented to Professor John Butt*. Edinburgh: John Donald, p.139.

opportunities for new products, processes, materials, markets and forms of organisation. It is the entrepreneurial function (whether implemented by an individual or organisation) to envision these opportunities and realise them through the development of innovations. Widespread diffusion of these innovations is the main source of long-term economic growth.

However, the process is not linear. For example, technical change often leads to scientific advance; production of goods and services often leads to learning which results in further technical change; etc. Further-more, the process is embedded in institutions that shape the evolving process itself. But institutions are themselves the outcome of political processes which are expressions of political power. Of particular interest here are financial institutions and therefore the rest of this section will focus on these institutions.

One of the main functions of banking financial institutions lies in the provision of credit which facilitates the growth of trade and industry (by allowing the recipients of the credit to buy goods and services before having sold their own). Credit is also an essential facilitator of the activities of entrepreneurs, as Joseph Schumpeter emphasised.

As Schumpeter (1934) noted, "…the entrepreneur…does need credit…in order to produce at all, to be able to carry out his new combinations [i.e. his/her innovations], to *become* an entrepreneur" (p.102). "The essential function of credit", Schumpeter argues, "consists in enabling the entrepreneur to withdraw the producers' goods which he needs from their previous employments, by exercising a demand for them, and thereby to force the economic system into new channels" (p.106). Given the availability of credit, Schumpeter observes, "The entrepreneurial function is not, in principle, connected with the possession of wealth…even though the accidental fact of the possession of wealth constitutes a practical advantage" (p.101).

A further function of financial institutions, one that is emphasised in this book, lies in the mobilisation of savings and the allocation of these savings to particular borrowers. At first the banks played the major role in this process but later other specialist financial institutions emerged that also played this role while providing coupled services. Particularly important in the Scottish case are insurance companies (especially life) and specialist investment managers (such as Baillie Gifford). The investment of the mobilised savings in existing and new activities further drives the process of economic growth. It is therefore important to understand the evolution of the institutions that shape the mobilisation and allocation of savings.

LONG WAVES OF TECHNICAL, ECONOMIC AND FINANCIAL CHANGE

Schumpeter (1939) argued that history is punctuated by particular junctures during which clusters of interrelated radical technical changes occur.[26] During these periods new products, processes, industries and markets emerge, replacing, displacing and merging with existing ones. By creating new opportunities, and with complementing and substituting effects, these periods stimulate economic growth. Christopher Freeman has analysed in detail these long waves of technical and economic change, identifying five waves that have occurred since the Industrial Revolution.[27] These are shown in Exhibit 2.1.

Freeman's colleague, Carlotta Perez (2002), has written about the behaviour of financial markets during these waves.[28] Essentially, her argument is that financial markets facilitate the emergence of the new wave of technical and economic activity by funding the entrepreneurial and other related economic activity that occurs. However, inevitably, the enthusiasm engendered as finance is allocated to the new activities turns into mania as those with funds to allocate become increasingly desperate to jump on board the bandwagon and join in the paper profits that are being made. But this leads only to irrational exuberance and the bubble

---

[26] Schumpeter, J.A. 1939. *Business Cycles: A Theoretical, Historical and Statistical Analysis of the Capitalist Process*, 2 vols. New York: McGraw-Hill.

[27] See, for example, Freeman, C. and Louçã, F. 2002. *As Time Goes By: From the Industrial Revolutions to the Information Revolution*. Oxford: Oxford University Press.

[28] Perez, C. 2002. *Technological Revolutions and Financial Capital*. Cheltenham: Edward Elgar.

Exhibit 2.1. Technical change and economic growth: five periods

Date	Age	Events	Industries
From 1771	'Industrial Revolution'	Arkwright's water-frame mill opens in Cromford; Watt's steam engine; Crompton's spinning mule	Mechanised textile industry; machinery
From 1829	Steam and Railways	Stephenson's 'Rocket' steam locomotive wins contest for Liverpool-Manchester railway; steam power applied to many industries (including textiles)	Railways; steam engines; iron and coal-mining; telegraph
From 1875	Steel, Electricity, Heavy Engineering	Carnegie's Bessemer steel plant opens in Pittsburg; steam engines for steel ships; electrical equipment; copper cables	Steel; steam-driven steel ships; electricity; telephone
From 1908	Oil, Cars, Mass Production	First Model-T produced by Ford in Detroit; internal combustion engine; oil and oil fuels; rubber; home electrical appliances	Mass-produced cars; oil; petrochemicals; rubber; home electrical products
From 1948	Information and Telecommunications	Shockley's transistor; computers; telecoms equipment; Intel's microprocessor; networked computing	Telecoms equipment and networks; computers; semiconductors and devices; software; consumer electronics; Internet

Source: Adapted from Perez (2002) and Fransman (various).

behaviour that Kindleberger (2000) has analysed that, in turn, results in panic and bust.[29] The question that remains, however, is whether the relationship between financial markets and real markets for goods and services can be modified so as to avoid the excesses of boom and bust that have characterised the five long waves to the present.

FROM 1771: THE INDUSTRIAL REVOLUTION

Textiles

In the mid-1700s linen became Scotland's premier industry, growing at a rapid rate. Linen had long been important in the Scottish economy. In 1587 King James VI had passed an Act providing incentives for Flemish flax growers to come to Scotland to assist in the development of the linen industry by teaching flax growing and spinning methods. It is thought that Robert Fleming, founder of the first Scottish investment trust, was a descendant of early Flemish immigrants. Indeed, Robert's father worked in the linen industry and went on to establish his own lint mill involved in the early stages of the processing of flax into linen.[30] From around 1740 to 1770 the output of linen quadrupled.

The British Linen Company

In 1746 the British Linen Company was created, later becoming Scotland's third public bank (with the Bank of Scotland and the Royal Bank). Although the tobacco trade, together with other trade with America and the Caribbean, was booming at this stage, industry was developing at a far slower pace. Linen manufacture (made by handloom) was the most important industrial activity but in Scotland it was still not well-developed. There were those who believed that government assistance was needed. Amongst these was a lawyer-landowner from Edinburgh, Andrew

---

[29] Kindleberger, C.P. 2000. *Manias, Panics and Crashes: A history of financial crises*. Basingstoke, Hampshire: Palgrave.
[30] Smith, B. 2000. *Robert Fleming, 1845-1933*. Haddington, Scotland: Whittinghame House, pp.3-6.

Fletcher (Lord Milton). He was chief adviser to the Whig Lord Islay (the Duke of Argyll) and both men were active in the establishment of the Royal Bank of Scotland, Lord Islay becoming its first Governor. Under pressure from Milton, the Board of Trustees for Manufactures was established. Milton became chairman of the Board's linen committee.

In about 1727 Milton motivated the formation of the Edinburgh Linen Co-Partnery. In the west of Scotland the successful Linen Society of Glasgow had been established, providing a source of out-going exports for the Glasgow merchants importing tobacco. In 1744, with the moral and financial support of the Governor of the Royal Bank, Lord Islay, and other landed and business men (some of whom were from London), Milton extended the scope of the Co-Partnery by entering into banking activities. In order to gain the right to bank and limit the liability of the partners it was decided to apply for a Royal Charter as had been given earlier to the Bank of Scotland and the Royal Bank. As Checkland (1975) notes:

> "Though Whig grandees were prominent among the promoters, the fact that the Company was Scottish was carefully muted by the use of the word British, in order to avoid the Jacobite taint. This had the further advantage that the Company, unlike the two public banks, could carry on its business anywhere in the Kingdom. The political power that had helped the Royal Bank into existence in 1727 was again successful. On 5 July 1746, the King signed and sealed the charter of the British Linen Company".[31]

Devine (1999) has pointed out that the British Linen Company "…was the only British chartered bank in the eighteenth century devoted specifically to the encouragement of industry".[32] Unlike the other two public banks it was able to trade as well as bank. It gave credit to flax weavers and spinners and encouraged them to improve their techniques and introduce new kinds of cloth.

---

[31] Checkland (1975), p.95.
[32] Devine (1999), p.106.

However, its influence on the linen industry was short-lived, its main impact being made from 1746 to 1753. Thereafter, the board of directors shifted emphasis away from the linen trade in favour of banking activities.[33]

As a result, it was cotton that was the first beneficiary of the Industrial Revolution. As Devine (1999) explains:

"Cotton achieved key technological advances with the adoption of the inventions from England of Hargreave's 'spinning jenny', Arkwright's waterframe and, above all, Crompton's 'mule'. When this last innovation was linked to James Watt's steam engine, the cotton factories were liberated from the need to be close to sources of water power and could instead concentrate on a much bigger scale in towns and cities".[34]

In 1826 it was estimated that over 250,000 people worked in textiles (cotton, linen and wool), of whom 60% were employed in cotton. At this time only 13,000 were employed in the iron trade and a further 19,000 in other manufactures.[35] A pattern of specialised geographical clustering had emerged with cotton manufacture concentrated in Glasgow, Paisley and the western lowlands, woollens based in the Borders and linen located in Dundee. [As will be seen later, linen production in Dundee evolved into jute production in the mid-1800s. It was through the investing of the surplus earned in jute manufacture and trade that the activities of Robert Fleming took shape.]

Why Edinburgh rather than Glasgow?

We are now in a position to answer the question posed by Charles Munn (1994), namely "…why so many financial institutions were head-quartered in Edinburgh rather than Glasgow" despite the economic dominance of the latter.[36] No doubt Munn is correct

---

[33] Checkland (1975), pp.96-7.
[34] Devine (1999), pp.108-9.
[35] ibid, p.109.
[36] Munn (1994), p.138.

when he points out that: "Ultimately the answer may be found in the eighteenth century rather than the nineteenth".[37]

Munn notes that all three of the Edinburgh public banks opened branches in Glasgow, the Royal Bank's being established in 1783 (later becoming that city's dominant bank) and the Bank of Scotland's being set up in 1787. Although with the emergence of the age of steam and railways from 1829 several new banks were set up in Glasgow (as we shall see), the Edinburgh banks, already both financially and politically dominant, were able to counter the threat and continue to provide banking services that adequately catered for the needs of Glasgow's business people.

Lothian husbandry

However, the Industrial Revolution was not only about factories but also influenced farming. The Lothian countryside surrounding Edinburgh was an important beneficiary. As Smout (1969) has pointed out, in the Lothians:

> "...farmers and landowners were trying their hand at new techniques and introducing new crops, like clover and turnips, that enabled them to send more beasts to the Falkirk tryst for sale to the English drovers. They were using improved implements, like the handy iron plough invented by the Berwickshire farmer James Small, and enclosing and dividing the landscape into its modern pattern of compact fields, windbreaks, woods and individual stone-built farms. Only in a very few areas had this process gone far enough to create a real 'revolution' in rural life. It had probably gone furthest in the Lothians, on some estates of the north-east and on the black-cattle lands in Ayrshire and Dumfriesshire".[38]

---

[37] ibid, p.139.
[38] Smout (1969), p.228.

FROM 1829: STEAM AND RAILWAYS

Use of Steam Engines

Having been the main engine of the first Industrial Revolution, by the 1850s cotton spinning was in a state of serious decline due largely to foreign competition. However, some of the technologies that fuelled the textile revolution (not only in cotton but also in linen and, to a lesser extent, wool) had been adopted and improved in order to drive new industries. One of the sources of technological continuity and progress was provided by the steam engine.

Steam engines were first developed to drive pumping mechanisms designed to alleviate flooding problems in mines. Thomas Savery and Thomas Newcomen's steam engines were designed for this purpose. In 1691 Savery made a vacuum steam engine. This was improved by Newcomen whose first working engine was installed at a coalmine in Staffordshire in 1712. In 1765 James Watt (born in Greenock, near Glasgow) modified Newcomen's design by developing an external condenser steam engine which he patented in 1769. In 1785 Edmund Cartwright invented the power loom that used the steam engine.

Soon the steam engine was being used to power boats. The era of the steamboat began in America in 1787 when John Fitch (1743-1798) carried out the first successful trial of a 45-foot steamboat on the Delaware River. In 1802, William Symington's steamboat, the Charlotte Dundas, was used as a tugboat on the Forth-Clyde canal (in 1789 his first experimental steamboat having operated successfully on the same canal). Robert Fulton (born in 1765 in Pennsylvania) is credited with turning the steamboat into a commercial success when in 1807 his Clermont went from New York City to Albany.

In 1804, Richard Trevithick (1771-1833), who designed the first steam engine locomotive for use on tramways first operated his vehicle in Wales. In 1814 George Stephenson built his first locomotive for the Stockton-Darlington Railway Line. In 1825, the Stockton & Darlington Railroad Company started the first railroad to carry goods and passengers on regular schedules. It used a steam locomotive designed by Stephenson who is considered to be the inventor of the first steam locomotive engine for railways (Trevithick's was designed for use on a road). Between 1826-29 Stephenson with his son designed the 'Rocket' steam locomotive that in 1829 won the contest for the Liverpool-Manchester Railway. The second 'long wave' – the Age of Steam and Railways – had arrived.

The Steam Transportation Innovation System

Rather than a stand-alone component, the steam engine should be seen as part of an evolving steam transportation innovation system. The components of this system interacted and evolved, driven both by learning and the new knowledge that it produced as well as by the market demands for its products and services.

The Glasgow area became a key global location for the cluster of activities that together produced the evolving steam transport system. In this area emerged the engineering skills, after a long process of competence accumulation that, as we have seen, went back to mining steam pumps, not only to produce steam engines of various kinds to power textile machinery, railway locomotives and steamboats, but also complementary components of the system such as coal, iron and boilers. Innovation in some components of the system stimulated linked innovations in others.

For example, a key innovation was made by James Beaumont Neilson (1792-1865) whose hot-blast process revolutionised iron production. Some of the innovations were essentially organisational in nature. One instance is the family firm established by David Napier. At its Camlachie foundry, engineered marine components and shipbuilding were combined within a single firm through a process of vertical integration.

The technological/competence continuity in the transition from textiles to steam transportation was evident in the geographical location of the clustered activities. As Devine (1999) observed: "What is striking...is that virtually all these engineering [ship firms] were clustered in the cotton districts of Glasgow, such as Tradeston and Camlachie. The close connection between the textile industries of the first Industrial Revolution and later fame in shipbuilding in the west of Scotland was confirmed".[39]

The global competitiveness that was soon achieved by the Glasgow-based Steam Transportation Innovation System is remarkable:

"By 1913, Glasgow and its satellite towns in the surrounding region of intensive industrialization produced one-half of British marine-engine horsepower, one-third of the railway locomotives and rolling stock, one-third of the shipping tonnage and about a fifth of the steel. On the eve of the First World War the Clyde not only built one-third of British output but almost a fifth of the world's tonnage, a record that was greater at the time by a considerable margin than all the German yards combined. At the heart of the heavy industrial complex with its world-wide markets was the huge range of engineering specialisms in engines, pumps, hydraulic equipment, railway rolling stock and a host of other products.

"Three of the four greatest firms building locomotives were in Glasgow; in 1903 they came together to form the North British Locomotive Works, 'the Titan of its trade' with a capacity to produce no fewer than 800 locomotives every year. This made the city the biggest locomotive-manufacturing centre in Europe, with engines being produced in large numbers for the Empire, South America and continental countries".[40]

The Co-evolution of Financial Institutions

As Checkland (1975) has observed:

"By 1930, the leading citizens of Glasgow were proud to call their burgh the second commercial city of the British Empire. But they were not pleased with its place in the banking world, being still under tutelage to Edinburgh.

---

[39] Devine (1999), p.257.
[40] ibid, pp.249-50.

No Glasgow bank had national status within Scotland, let alone Britain. The total number of partners in the Ship, the Thistle and the Glasgow Bank did not exceed thirty persons in all... On the other hand, no less than nine non-Glasgow banks had branches in the city. To a large extent the profits on banking and the premiums on the increased values of bank shares went to Edinburgh, just as they had in 1750. There was a feeling in Glasgow that the Edinburgh banks...were too much pre-occupied with banking safety, holding too large a part of their loanable resources in the form of securities rather than extending discounts and advances to support commerce and industry".[41]

In response to this sentiment, several new banks were established in Glasgow in the 1830s in order to redress the perceived imbalance. However, while the needs of the upper echelons of the Steam Transportation Innovation System appear to have been adequately served by the existing Edinburgh-dominated banks, lesser interests responded to the uneven development by starting their own banks that they hoped would result in more resources being channelled to them.

These banks included the Glasgow Union Banking Company, started in 1830 by Robert Stewart, a wine merchant, and "...other Glasgow men of business...partly in an effort to arrest the emigration [of the city's economic activity] westwards [where activities related to the steam transportation system were located]".[42] Similarly, the Western Bank of Scotland was set up in 1833 by a second group of Glasgow businessmen who "...decided that the holding of a large reserve in the form of securities or London balances, as practiced by the Edinburgh banks, was inappropriate to the needs of Glasgow and the west".[43]

Likewise, in 1838 the Clydesdale Bank was created by "...a group of Glasgow businessmen of the middling order, liberal-radicals who had helped to carry through parliamentary and

---

[41] Checkland (1975), p.326.
[42] ibid, p.326.
[43] ibid, p.327.

municipal reform in the early 1830s and who were active in the government and charities of the city".[44] The Clydesdale "…was a thoroughly middle-class bank, its directors were men of modest business scale. It broke with the custom of having a landed aristocrat as governor, but was content with a chairman of its own kind".[45] Finally, there was the City of Glasgow Bank, launched in 1839 on the grounds that there remained demand in Glasgow for a fourth bank.

However, these banks were not large or successful enough to seriously challenge the Edinburgh banks. In 1843 the Union Bank of Scotland was formed (incorporating the Glasgow Union Bank, 1830, the remnants of the Ship Bank, 1750 and the Thistle Bank, 1761).[46] In 1857 the Western Bank failed as did the City of Glasgow Bank in 1878 (whose collapse would provoke one of the most important financial crises in 19th century Britain[47]). By 1880, Checkland (1975) concludes:

"…though Glasgow…continued as a vigorous centre of banking, the Glasgow challenge for Scottish banking leader-ship, so vigorously begun in the 1830s, was ended. Dominance by Edinburgh, threatened for some forty years, was successfully reasserted, with five banking head offices against Glasgow's two. With the Western and the City of Glasgow banks liquidated, there was to be no more irresponsible behaviour in the west; neither was there to be any initiative capable of breaking out of a pattern that was fast hardening".[48]

---

[44] ibid, p.335.

[45] ibid, p.337.

[46] The Union Bank of Scotland in 1955 became part of the Bank of Scotland.

[47] See Collins and Baker (2003), pp.91-7.

[48] Checkland (1975), pp.496-7.

RAILWAYS AND BRITISH INVESTMENT

Investment Trusts

The advent of railways initiated the second wave of economic activity by creating new opportunities for investment. Scottish manufacturing firms, as we have seen, particularly in Glasgow and the west of Scotland, were transformed. But so were Scottish financial institutions. The activities of Scottish commercial banks were examined in earlier sections. Here attention will be paid to a new category of financial institution, namely investment trusts.

The Foreign & Colonial Government Trust

The Foreign & Colonial Government Trust was launched on 19 March 1868.[49] It initiated an important financial innovation. The basic idea was simple; by pooling resources, smaller savers, with the guidance of experienced professionals, would be able to do collectively what they could not do individually, namely earn a premium risk-adjusted rate of return on their savings over and above that available on alternative domestic financial assets such as consols and bank deposits.

Of course, the commercial bank itself was in many respects a similar innovation. The commercial bank was also an institution that could do collectively for savers and depositors what they could not do for themselves, namely increase the risk-adjusted return on their savings and deposits. As an institution, the commercial bank was able to develop special competencies, embodied in banking practices and routines, to evaluate the returns that could be made from loans to various kinds of borrowers, including assessing the risks involved and monitoring the performance of the loan.[50]

---

[49] The present account draws heavily on Newlands, J. 1997. *Put Not Your Trust in Money: A history of the investment trust industry from 1868 to the present day*. London: Chappin Kavanagh.

[50] As economists such as Joseph Stiglitz have emphasised, competencies such as these have been necessary as a result of information asymmetries, namely the lender not having as much information as the borrower regarding matters such as the borrower's intentions, the uses to which the loan will be put, the returns to these uses and the risks involved. Under such conditions, Stiglitz points out, markets and prices do not provide a sufficient solution to the problems raised;

Furthermore, by lending to large numbers of borrowers, commercial banks were able to reduce risk by spreading it. Although commercial banking began historically as an additional set of activities undertaken by existing businesses – the goldsmiths being the obvious example – the competencies and scale needed soon resulted in the emergence of commercial banks as a specialised institution, as was seen earlier in this chapter with the emergence of commercial banking in Scotland.

A key additional ingredient offered by the Foreign & Colonial Government Trust, and the other imitation trusts that were established as the innovation diffused, was higher returns that came from investments in overseas markets where market rates of return were significantly higher than in the UK. Wealthy investors had sufficient resources to create substantial portfolios that would allow them to take advantage of the higher returns while lowering risks by spreading it. Investment trusts, by pooling the funds of smaller savers, were able to offer similar advantages. The objective was succinctly explained in the Foreign & Colonial Government Trust's first prospectus: "To provide the investor of moderate means the same advantage as the large capitalist in diminishing risk in Foreign & Colonial stocks by spreading the investment over a number of stocks".[51] While in 1868 consols yielded 3.3%, Foreign & Colonial promised an expected yield of 7%.[52]

However, in order to secure the inflow of funds from savers needed to finance the purchase of foreign stocks and in order to deliver the promised yield, two major problems had to be overcome, both relating to information asymmetries. First, potential savers had to be convinced that those who wielded power in Foreign & Colonial were people of integrity who were taking all reasonable steps to secure the promised higher returns. However, the job of convincing at this juncture was not particularly easy. Just

---

for example, auction markets cannot be used to allocate scarce loans to would-be borrowers based on the highest price offered. Institutions that go beyond pure market transactions are therefore necessary. See Greenwald, B. and Stiglitz, J.E. 1992. 'Information, Finance and Markets: The architecture of allocative mechanisms'. In V. Zamagni (ed), *Finance and the Enterprise*. London: Academic Press, pp.11-36.

[51] Newlands (1997), p.15.

[52] ibid, pp.15 and 13.

two years before, in 1866, the Overend & Gurney bank had collapsed, the incident being referred to as "...the greatest financial strain the City had experienced, in time of peace".[53] Of course, financial scandals were well known at the time. Lacking full information, potential savers needed reassurance.

This was provided in a number of ways. One crucial form of reassurance came through a complementary institutional innovation that had the effect of limiting the saver's overall liability and therefore exposure to risk.[54] This was the Companies Act of 1862 that made easier the establishment of limited liability companies, including finance companies.[55] Reassurance, and therefore trust, was also facilitated through the experience and reputation of the founders, the trust's Chairman and the trustees.

In the case of Foreign & Colonial, the three founders – Philip Rose, Samuel Laing and James Thompson Mackenzie – were all extremely well-known and well-connected and had all made substantial sums of money in the railway boom. Furthermore, they had all been involved for five years already in forming and managing the General Credit & Finance Company (GCFC), one of the first major finance companies to be established after the passage of the 1862 Companies Act. Indeed, it has been suggested that the kernel innovative idea behind the investment trust was already present in the GCFC. The first Chairman of Foreign & Colonial was Lord Westbury, who had been Solicitor-General, Attorney-General and Lord Chancellor. The other trustees included well-known MPs and a reputable banker.[56]

---

[53] ibid, p.8.

[54] This institutional innovation illustrates Douglas North's definition of an institution in terms of the rules of the game. North, D. 1990. *Institutions, Institutional Change and Economic Performance*. Cambridge: Cambridge University Press.

[55] The consequences of limiting liability, however, are complex, with upsides and downsides different for the various kinds of player involved; saver, shareholder, borrower or manager. In the case of a commercial bank, for instance, while shareholders may want to see their overall liabilities limited, savers may feel that this increases moral hazard, reducing pressure on managers, and therefore exposes them to more risk. In the case of investment trusts, however, savers were shareholders in one form or another.

[56] For further details, see Newlands (1997), chapters 1 and 3.

The past experience of the three founders in railways also helped to solve the second major information asymmetry problem confronted by Foreign & Colonial, namely sufficient information about expected investment returns and risks in foreign countries. Difficult as these issues are in one's own home country, the problems are compounded when information is required about foreign countries. These difficulties became painfully apparent in 1890 with the Baring Crisis when problems in Argentina engulfed one of the most prestigious merchant banks in the City of London, Baring Bros. & Co., provoking a further major financial crisis. James Mackenzie, one of Foreign & Colonial's founders, was Deputy Chairman of the East Bengal Railway.[57] In this way a major financial innovation was born.

Robert Fleming, jute and railways

The first investment trust in Scotland, signifying the widespread diffusion of this important financial innovation, was established by Robert Fleming in Dundee in 1873. The origins of this investment trust are rooted in jute and railways.

The Dundee area had by this time a long history in wool and linen production. The mechanisation of the textile industry having begun with cotton spinning had, with a lag, been extended to linen and Dundee had specialised in this area. Devine (1999) notes that jute was first sent to Dundee from Bengal by the East India Company in the hope that the cheapness of this fibre – used in products such as bagging and carpets – would prove attractive to Dundee's textile manufacturers:[58]

> "Dundee was the first to solve the technical problem of the dryness and brittleness of the new fibre, not only because the city and the surrounding region specialised in coarser linens, but because raw jute was softened by the process of 'batching' or the application of a mix of whale

---

[57] ibid, p.10.
[58] According to Smith (2000), p.12, the jute industry was introduced into Dundee in 1822 but only became a significant activity in the 1830s.

oil and water. Since the later eighteenth century Dundee had become a leading whaling centre in Scotland".[59]

One of the firms that made the switch from coarse linens to jute was Cox Brothers & Co. who ran a mill in the village of Lochee near Dundee. It was in this village that Robert Fleming was born, although the family moved to Dundee the following year.[60]

In 1861, at the age of 15, Robert Fleming took up his second job, this time with Cox Brothers.[61] When he joined Cox the company was growing rapidly and was very profitable, partly because of the lucrative business it had done with both sides during the American Civil War in supplying jute products such as sand bags and supply bags. Cox's Camperdown Works in Lochee covered "...about fourteen acres, the works were driven by steam engines of 1,335 horse-power (a very large capacity in those days) and had a labour force of over 3,200".[62]

It was at Cox Brothers that Fleming began to take a close interest in the stock market. In 1866, however, Fleming became technically insolvent when a bank in which he had put savings was forced to close in the aftermath of the Overend, Gurney & Co. financial crisis. Although he lost the money he had invested he was also liable to meet calls on the bank's unpaid capital. Since this was money he did not have, "...he was forced to compromise with the liquidator". Embarrassed, he vowed to repay the money when he could and this he was able to do within five years. In the same year he left Cox Brothers and joined the leading jute firm in Dundee, Baxter Brothers & Co.[63]

---

[59] Devine (1999), p.256.

[60] Robert's father, John, worked for a while in the Tay works of the jute spinning and weaving factory of Gilroy Brothers & Co. that was to become the world's second-largest jute companies after Cox Brothers. Smith (2000), p.7.

[61] He started his first job at the age of 13 in 1859 with James Ramsay, a prominent Dundee merchant. ibid, p.10.

[62] ibid, p.13.

[63] Smith (2000) comments: "It is impossible to tell whether the move [from Cox to Baxter] was linked in any way to his financial misfortune. It may be that by then he had decided that it was time to seek further experience elsewhere and seized the opportunity when it presented itself. On the other hand it is possible that he felt too embarrassed to stay on in the office of Cox Brothers or he may

Edward Baxter, who ran the company when Fleming joined, started a business with his father exporting directly to overseas markets rather than going through Liverpool and London as until then had been the usual practice. They also established one of the earliest flax spinning mills in Dundee. In 1831 they had given up the mill in order to focus on their trading interests. Baxter had done a good deal of trade with America and from 1818 he had acted as the American Vice-Consul in Dundee.[64] His trading interests had made him aware of investment opportunities overseas and he had become an expert in overseas investment, his investments including holdings in railway companies in the United States and Latin America "…with only a sprinkling of British stocks".[65]

As a clerk in Baxter's office, Fleming was able to learn about overseas investments, particularly in the United States. Ironically, when Baxter died in July 1871 Fleming's learning opportunities increased. The net assets in Baxter's estate amounted to half a million pounds (currently worth more than £30 million) and included American securities. Fleming was asked by the trustees of Baxter's estate to assist in the management of the trust that was established. Although there is no evidence that he played a major role in the management of the trust's investments, these transactions being carried out by Baxter's investment bankers in the United States, it is clear that this was an important learning opportunity for Fleming.[66]

At any rate, even though there is no conclusive evidence regarding whether Fleming made his first visit to the US in 1870 on behalf of Baxter and returned very impressed with the opportunities available to British investors,[67] it is clear that by at

---

have been asked to leave. Victorian employers did not take kindly to clerks who got themselves into financial difficulties" (p.16).

[64] ibid, p.17.

[65] ibid, p.17.

[66] ibid, pp.18-9.

[67] According to Newlands (1997), "In 1870…Baxter sent Robert Fleming to the United States to represent him on company business" (pp.56-7). However, Smith (2000), Fleming's posthumous official biographer, states that "…no evidence has been uncovered to confirm that Fleming visited America on behalf of Edward Baxter in 1870, returning 'very impressed with the importance of the

least the first few years of the 1870s Fleming had come up with the idea of establishing an investment trust in Dundee using the Foreign & Colonial as a model. His intention was to draw on the savings pool that had accumulated in Dundee largely through the jute trade.

The Scottish American Investment Trust, Scotland's first investment trust, was established at the initial formal meeting of the trustees held on 1 February 1873 in the offices of the jute tycoon, Thomas Cox (who was responsible for the Cox family's financial affairs). The minutes of the meeting record that: "It was proposed to consider the establishment of a Trust similar in principle to the Foreign & Colonial established in London by Lord Westbury".[68] Highlighting the importance of problems of asymmetric information in taking advantage of the potentially high returns available from investments in the United States (referred to earlier), the trust's prospectus read:

"There is probably no field for Investment wider, or combining in a greater degree the elements of security and profit than the United States, but the difficulties which individual investors in this country experience in obtaining reliable information regarding American securities prevent their availing themselves of the opportunities which they offer.

"Through the medium of the present Trust, these difficulties are removed, and home investors may obtain an interest in a wide and careful selection of American Railroad and other Bonds, at the minimum of trouble, and with the maximum of security and profit".[69]

Fleming became Secretary of the trust, retaining this position for fifteen years until he moved to London. However, his key contribution came in the form of his distinctive knowledge of the United States, particularly in the area of railroads (and the people

---

USA and the opportunities for the investment of British capital', as was stated in Fleming's obituary in The Times of 2nd August 1933..." (p.19).

[68] Newlands (1997), p.59.

[69] Smith (2000), p.27.

and institutions that facilitated investments in this field). In the course of his business life it was calculated that he made 64 trips across the Atlantic.[70] Fleming became an internationally renowned expert in railroads in the United States and their financing (and refinancing when they got into trouble).

Apart from Thomas Cox there were three other trustees – John Guild, Thomas Smith and John Sharp. All were well-connected in Dundee's business community. Cox, Smith and Sharp were all involved in the jute industry at the head of important spinning and manufacturing firms. Smith had also been employed by Edward Baxter, like Fleming, and Guild was a partner with his brother in a large firm with shipping interests.[71] The launch was extremely successful and the trust's bank, the "...British Linen Bank, was flooded with applications, to such an extent that to meet the demand for shares it was decided to withdraw the prospectus and print a new one with a [higher] capital issue...".[72]

William Menzies and Edinburgh's first investment trust

Scotland's second investment trust, Edinburgh's first, was established by William John Menzies. The Scottish American Investment Company Limited, often referred to as SAINTS (a company with a name very similar to Robert Fleming's trust), was set up in Edinburgh on 29 March 1873.

William Menzies was born in 1834, the son of Allan Menzies, a Writer to the Signet who from 1847 to 1856 was Professor of Conveyancing at the University of Edinburgh.[73] In 1858 he became a Writer to the Signet and in the 1860s he established his own law practice in Edinburgh.

---

[70] ibid, p.2.

[71] ibid, p.26.

[72] As recollected by Fleming, ibid, p.28.

[73] The information in this section comes largely from Slaven, A. and Checkland, S. (eds). 1990. *Dictionary of Scottish Business Biography, Vol. 2: Processing, Distribution, Services*. Aberdeen: Aberdeen University Press, pp.414-5. This section on Menzies was written by Ronald Weir, the biographer of the Scottish American Investment Company Limited. See also Weir, R.B. 1973. *A History of the Scottish American Investment Company Limited 1873-1973*. Edinburgh; and Jackson, W.T. 1968. *The Enterprising Scot: Investors in the American West after 1873*. Edinburgh.

As with many lawyers in Edinburgh who regarded themselves as 'men of affairs'[74] rather than as professionals concerned exclusively with narrow legal issues, Menzies' interactions with his clients included advice on investment matters. On three occasions – in 1864, 1867 and 1872 – the affairs of his clients took him to the United States where he was impressed by the opportunities offered.[75] The investment trust that he founded was designed to help both him and his clients benefit from these opportunities in the United States.

As with Foreign & Colonial in London and Robert Fleming's first investment trust in Dundee, Menzies succeeded in involving a group of influential local dignitaries. Sir George Warrender, a baronet and a director of the Royal Bank of Scotland, became chairman of the trust's board. Two board members controlled important local firms (in paper-making and publishing, one of whom was Menzies' uncle); one was an Edinburgh architect; one was head of an Edinburgh firm of solicitors; one represented an American banking firm; and the last was the consulting engineer to the Caledonian Railway Company who offered expertise in evaluating new development in American railroads. Menzies' brother became secretary to the new company. Furthermore, in order to deal with the problem of information about investments in the United States an advisory board was established in America consisting mainly of fellow Scots he had met on his visits.[76]

By the 1890s Menzies was regarded as an international expert on American finance and investment: "This accumulated expertise contrasts with his very limited knowledge of American investments prior to the flotation of Scottish American. His initial portfolio selection was based on the *Financial Chronicle*, the *Railway Magazine* and a railroad map of the United States!".[77] During his life he made a total of 35 visits to the United States. The Scottish

---

[74] According to Gavin Gemmell, former senior partner at Baillie Gifford, the phrase 'men of affairs' was traditionally common amongst Edinburgh lawyers. Interview with Gavin Gemmell.

[75] Slaven and Checkland (1990), p.414.

[76] ibid, p.414.

[77] ibid, p.415.

American Investment Company Limited immediately became an extremely successful company, a success story that continued.[78]

Edinburgh's social structure

The story of William Menzies and SAINTS illustrates the social structure that existed in Edinburgh in the latter part of the 19th century. Recalling Checkland's (1975) succinct summary, Edinburgh from the mid-1700s, "...though no longer a political capital...was still the centre for the nobility and the landed men, and for the law courts and the church. In finance, the Bank of Scotland and the Royal Bank had established themselves in the centre of Scottish life, sustained by their associates, the Edinburgh private banks. It was upon Edinburgh that landed savings converged, as did landed borrowings, still the largest elements in the nation's credit transactions".[79]

Clearly, Edinburgh was a professional city to an extent that Glasgow was not. This emerges from Exhibits 2.2 and 2.3 which show the professional composition of both cities.

As Exhibit 2.2 clearly shows, Edinburgh in the late-18th century was dominated by nobles, gentry and professionals who together accounted for more than one-third of the city's population. In Glasgow, by contrast, it was the merchants, manufacturers and petit bourgeois traders, artisans and craftsmen who dominated. This class structure continued into the 19th century as shown in Exhibit 2.3.

---

[78] At the end of 2003, the management contract for the Scottish American Investment Trust Company (SAINTS), which had previously been managed by First State Investments, was awarded to Baillie Gifford. *The Scotsman*, 10 December 2003.

[79] Checkland (1975), pp.107-8.

Exhibit 2.2. Workforce by occupation in Edinburgh and Glasgow, late-18th century

Occupation	Edinburgh 1773/74 (%)	Glasgow 1783/84 (%)
Nobles and gentry	5.4	1.0
Professional men	28.8	12.3
Merchants and manufacturers	12.5	30.0
Small tradesmen, artisans, craftsmen, etc.	30.5	42.1

Source: Smout (1969), p.357.

The most striking aspect of Exhibit 2.3 is the contrast between Edinburgh and Glasgow in terms of the weight of professional and industrial employment. Also of interest is the gender breakdown of the figures. While in 1841 13% of Edinburgh's male workforce consisted of professionals (though only 2% of its female workers), the corresponding figures for Glasgow were 5% and 1% respectively. However, male industrial workers in Glasgow made up 74% of workers (female industrial workers 65%) compared to Edinburgh's 62% and only 24% respectively. Also indicative of the predominance of the upper and middle classes is domestic employment which employed 70% of Edinburgh's women workers, while only 32% in Glasgow (7% of Edinburgh's males compared to only 2% in Glasgow). Interestingly, the figures for commercial, and agriculture and fishing are very similar in both cities.

Exhibit 2.3. Workforce by occupation in Edinburgh and Glasgow, 1841

Occupation	Edinburgh and Suburbs (%)	Glasgow and Suburbs (%)
Professional		
M	13	5
F	2	1
Industrial		
M	62	74
F	24	65
Commercial		
M	14	15
F	3	3
Agriculture & Fishing		
M	3	4
F	1	0.5
Domestic		
M	7	2
F	70	32

Source: Devine (1999), p.161.

Lawyers as a social category in Edinburgh are of particular interest, not only because of the role that they played professionally, politically and socially but also because – as the case of William Menzies clearly illustrates and the detailed examination of Baillie Gifford to be presented below will confirm – they also played a key role in the evolution of Edinburgh's (and Scotland's) financial institutions. By the 18th century their role had already been established. As Smout (1969) observed:

"The [Edinburgh] lawyers' closest links...were with the country gentry of the Lothians rather than with the 'mercantile interest' of their own city. Every advocate or writer who made a success of his calling sought an estate in East Lothian or Midlothian, or even further afield: it was an excellent investment, and it conferred upon his family the political privilege and social prestige that all landowners relished. Conversely, landowners over-burdened with children found themselves mulling over the advantages of a career at the Scottish bar for a younger son. Or of a lawyer as a husband for a favourite daughter. So general was intermarriage and exchange of personnel between lawyers and gentlemen that they came to treat one another as perfect equals....

"The lawyers included many who were among the most intelligent and enthusiastic intellects in Scotland. They were highly trained, some having attended a continental university...broadly read...politically well-connected...involved in making and executing economic policy.... They were the backbone of the city's innumerable clubs and societies...they formed a cultural elite".[80]

Supporting this description, Exhibit 2.4 shows the occupation of the fathers of Writers to the Signet from 1690 to 1829.

As Exhibit 2.4 shows, well over half of the fathers of Writers were landowners or lawyers, the latter becoming more important over time. As Smout (1969) comments, these figures represent "...no decline in the importance of the gentry: since the number of writers increased rapidly towards 1800, the absolute number of recruits from the landowning class probably did not fall at all. Rather it shows the success of those who exploited the new openings for the middle class in the period following the Union [of the parliaments in 1707]".[81] Also of interest is the significant increase in the categories army officer/colonial adventurer/civil servant and tenant-farmer, the latter referring largely to the

---

[80] Smout (1969), p.350.
[81] ibid, pp.351-2.

prosperous Lothian farmers discussed earlier. All these social groups, as we shall see, were important in the rise of Baillie Gifford.

Exhibit 2.4. Occupation of fathers of Edinburgh Writers to the Signet (300 Writers to the Signet, percentage)

Father's standing	Period in which writers qualified		
	1690-1749	1750-1789	1790-1829
Legal profession	22	20	30
Landowner	49	41	25
Minister	9	10	3
Army officer, colonial adventurer, civil service officer	3	1	10
Physician, teacher, architect	2	10	8
Tenant-farmer	1	3	9
Merchant	12	13	13
Tradesman	2	1	2
Unskilled labourer	-	1	-

Source: The Society of Writers to His Majesty's Signet, Edinburgh, 1936. Taken from Smout (1969), p.351.

The social composition of Edinburgh's population was both cause and effect of the city's dominance in Scotland, not only financially (though not economically) but also politically and culturally. With this population providing the nutritious soil it is no wonder that it was in Edinburgh, rather than Glasgow, that the Scottish Enlightenment emerged. As Smout (1969) describes the situation:

> "In the end both Hume and Smith and many like them spent much of their lives in Edinburgh. It is a fair guess that what Hume in another letter called 'good company' was the greatest allurement. Alexander Carlyle described how he and his friends, the cream of the university, the clergy, the lawyers and the visiting gentry, met in a city large enough to be diverse and small enough to be intimate".[82]

Scottish and English investment trusts

Information on the formation of investment trusts in England and Scotland up to 1890 is provided in Exhibit 2.5. It can be seen from Exhibit 2.5 that Scotland was a relatively fast adopter of investment trusts (judged in terms of the number of trusts established). Of the investment trusts established up to 1881, 25% were in Scotland (which had roughly 10% of the UK's population). However, between 1881 and 1890 the growth in investment trusts was much faster in England with the result that in 1890 Scotland had just under 10% of the combined investment trusts in England and Scotland.

Exhibit 2.6 shows the picture in 1935. By 1900 Scotland had almost 20% of the investment trusts in England and Scotland. From 1909 to 1923 there was a greater absolute number of investment trusts established in Scotland than in England. In 1931 Scotland had 38% of the total number of investment trusts in England and Scotland.

---

[82] ibid, p.477. For some recent studies of Edinburgh over this period see, Cosh (2003), Buchan (2003) and Herman (2002).

Exhibit 2.5. Trust companies operating in England and Scotland, 1890

Year formed	England (number)	Scotland (number)	Total
Before 1881	12	4	16
1881 – 1890	80	5	85
Total	**92**	**9**	**101**

Source: Calculated from Burton and Corner (1968), Table 3-1, p.28.

Exhibit 2.6. Age distribution of 209 investment trusts operating in 1935[1]

Year formed	England (number)	Scotland (number)	Total
Before 1901	47	11	58
1901 – 1908	5	4	9
1909 – 1914	6	17	23
1915 – 1923	8	3	11
1924 – 1931	64	44	108
Total	**130**	**79**	**209**

[1] Burton and Corner (1968) note that the 209 investment trusts on which data in this table are based are "good approximations" of "the actual number of companies formed" during this period (p.46). *Source*: Calculated from Burton and Corner (1968), Table 4-1, p.47.

In Exhibit 2.7 information is provided on the date of establishment of investment trusts according to Scottish city.

Exhibit 2.7. Formation of new Scottish investment trusts

First Dundee Investment Trust	1873
First Edinburgh Investment Trust	1873
First Glasgow Investment Trust	1907
First Aberdeen Investment Trust	1908
1909 – 1914	Edinburgh – 11 Aberdeen – 3 Glasgow – 2 Dundee – 1 **Total - 17**
1915 – 1930	Glasgow - 21 Edinburgh – 20 Aberdeen – 3 Dundee – 3 **Total – 47**

Source: Calculated from Burton and Corner (1968), p.47.

From Exhibit 2.7 the dominance of Edinburgh vis-à-vis Glasgow emerges clearly. While the first investment trust established in Edinburgh was founded in 1873 (by William Menzies, the same year that Robert Fleming set up Scotland's first investment trust), it was only in 1907 that Glasgow's first investment trust appeared. From 1909 to 1914 in Edinburgh 11 investment trusts were established, the corresponding figure for Glasgow being two. However, from 1915 to 1930, 21 investment trusts were set up in Glasgow compared to 20 in Edinburgh. These figures are hardly surprising in view of the dominance of Edinburgh as Scotland's major financial district from the 18th century, as documented earlier in this chapter.

The significance of British investment trusts
The role played by investment trusts in the mobilisation of UK savings relative to that of other financial institutions for the period 1903-33 is shown in Exhibit 2.8.

Exhibit 2.8. Assets of selected British financial institutions, 1903-33 (£ millions)

Date	Investment Trusts	Banks	Insurance Companies	Post Office Saving Banks	Trustee Saving Banks	Building Societies
1903	70.0	934.0	352.6	146.1	57.2	65.0
1913	90.0	1,205.0	530.1	187.4	68.7	65.3
1920	112.0	2,604.1	712.1	267.1	91.3	87.0
1933	295.6	2,697.8	1,449.6	326.7	171.4	501.1

Note that the figures for investment trusts are estimates.
Source: Cassis (1990), p.144.

Exhibit 2.8 shows that investment trusts played a relatively small part compared particularly to banks and insurance companies. Their assets in 1933 were only 11% of the former's and 20% of the latter's. From 1903 to 1920 the assets of the investment trusts exceeded those of the building societies and the trustee savings banks. However, in 1933, with the rapid growth of building societies in the intervening period, their assets significantly exceeded those of the investment trusts.

However, these figures conceal the distinctiveness of the investment trusts. Most significantly, the investment trusts were one of the most important vehicles for the export of British capital.

Indeed, Cassis (1990) notes that before 1914 investment trusts invested about 90% of their capital abroad and more than 50% during the greater part of the inter-war period.[83] They therefore made a significant contribution to the unprecedented proportion of its national savings that the UK was investing overseas. As one writer put it:

> "Great Britain's immense export of capital is among the most important events of the late nineteenth century. Rising in the 1850s and 1860s, the flow of net foreign investment averaged about a third of the nation's annual accumulations [of savings] from 1870 to 1914. As a result of the annual flows the stock of net overseas assets grew from around 7 percent of the stock of net national wealth in 1850 to around 14 percent in 1870 and then to around 32 percent in 1913. Never before or since has one nation committed so much of its national income and savings to capital formation abroad".[84]

Cassis (1990) also concludes that it is "...questionable whether [investment trusts] ever succeeded in attracting small investors for their shareholders belonged to the wealthy classes or, increasingly after 1914, became institutional investors, like insurance companies and, later, pension funds".[85]

SCOTLAND'S FAILURES AND SUCCESSES

Returning to Exhibit 2.1 which shows the five waves of inter-related technological and economic change since the Industrial Revolution, it is clear that Scotland did extremely well during the first two waves, the age of the industrial revolution and the age of steam and railways. However, it was with the third wave – the age of steel, electricity and heavy industry – that the Scottish performance began to falter. Although steel and heavy industry

---

[83] Cassis, Y. (1990), p.154.

[84] Edelstein (1994), p.173, quoted in Collins and Baker (2003), p.1.

[85] Cassis (1990), p.154.

were components of the steam transportation innovation system and therefore were reasonably well served by the competencies and infrastructure that had accumulated in Scotland, electricity (networks and equipment, including later consumer electrical appliances) was a different story based on a new technological paradigm. In the 1920s, for example, Scotland only contributed about 2% of total British output of electrical goods.[86] The same was true in the newly growing field of telephony.

Furthermore, as Devine (1999, 2003) has stressed, even during the first two waves the Scottish performance, though impressive, did not bring trickle-down improvements for the majority of the population. This is revealed most dramatically in the figures for emigration. Devine (1999) points out that:

"Not far short of 2 million people emigrated from Scotland overseas between 1830 and 1914 [currently the total population of Scotland is around 5 million], a rate of outward movement that was around one and a half times that of England and Wales. This did not include another 600,000 who moved south of the border. The haemorrhage was so great that it placed Scotland near the top of the European emigration league, along with Ireland and Norway.... Scotland was almost alone among European countries in having experienced both large-scale industrialization and a great outward movement of population".[87]

Together with emigration went low incomes and widespread poverty.

But it was with the fourth and fifth waves – the age of cars and mass production, and the age of information and communications – that Scotland fell even further behind. Perhaps the best indicator of Scotland's failure to keep up with the fourth and fifth waves is the absence of large Scottish frontier-leading companies in these

---

[86] Devine (1999), p.269.

[87] ibid, p.265.

fields.[88] The contrast with the presence of world-leading large Scottish companies in areas such as textiles, steam engines and shipbuilding during the first and second waves (as documented in this chapter) is striking.

Very different from the story of Scottish manufacturing, however, is the story of Scottish financial institutions. Most notably, Edinburgh's premier financial institutions continued their success, not only in Scotland and the rest of Britain but increasingly outside the UK as their activities expanded globally. Indeed, these institutions overcame the limitations of the domestic economy through the globalisation of their activities. The outstanding examples include the Royal Bank of Scotland, Standard Life and, in the area of independent fund managers, Baillie Gifford.

---

[88] For the very different story of Japan that, under very different circumstances, was able to catch up in the areas of information and communications and keep up, see Fransman (1995, 1999, 2002).

THE ORIGINS OF BAILLIE GIFFORD

1907-1913 – THE ORIGINS OF BAILLIE GIFFORD

Augustus Charles Baillie

Baillie Gifford was established as a law firm in 1907[1] after Augustus Charles Baillie invited the younger Thomas Johnstone Carlyle Gifford to join him in a partnership. Baillie was born in 1861, the son of Evan P. Montagu Baillie. We do not know anything about the background of Augustus Baillie's family nor about the profession of his father. However, we do know that Augustus Baillie was educated at Marlborough School and that in 1905 he married Meta Trotter, the daughter of Major-General Sir Henry Trotter whose family came from Mortonhall, Midlothian, and Charter Hall, Berwickshire.[2] The couple had one son and one daughter.

Baillie served in the South African War, 1899-1902 (the Anglo-Boer War), during which he commanded a column of mixed troops in the Cape Colony. He also served during the First World War, reaching the rank of Lieutenant-Colonel with the second regiment of the Second Lovat Scouts. In *Scottish Biographies*[3] (1938) he was listed as being a Member of the King's Bodyguard for Scotland (The Royal Company of Archers). His clubs were listed as Boodle's (London) and New (Edinburgh).

After school, Baillie qualified as a Notary Public (NP), a qualification that limited his right of practice as a lawyer. When he

---

[1] Its first financial year ended on 31 March 1908. Baillie died on 8 January 1939.

[2] http://freepages.genealogy.rootsweb.com/~trotter/trotter_of_mortonhall.htm.

[3] *Scottish Biographies*. 1938. Glasgow: Jackson, Son and Co.

returned from the South African War he established a law partnership with a lawyer named Fletcher whom he had known in Inverness-shire. The law practice was called Fletcher & Baillie, WS, and was located at 12 Hill Street in Edinburgh.

Their law firm did a good deal of estate and trust work, largely for aristocratic friends and rich relatives. In addition, they advised their clients regarding their investments. However, Fletcher died suddenly in 1906, leaving Baillie, with his limited legal qualification, looking for a suitable replacement who was qualified to practice law. He turned to a personal contact, Lyon Mackenzie, a member of the Bar, who subsequently consulted William Purves of Messrs W. & F. Haldane, WS. Through this network of private contacts Baillie was given the name of a 25-year-old Writer to the Signet, Carlyle Gifford. Gifford had had professional contact with Purves.

Thomas Johnstone Carlyle Gifford

Carlyle Gifford's father, Patrick Gifford, was born in Penninghame, Wigtown, in 1813.[4] Patrick Gifford's father, John Gifford, was a farmer.[5] Wigtown, on the coast, lies some forty kilometres west of Kirkcudbright and is south-west of Dumfries and Castle Douglas. By 1851, at the time of the Census of Scotland held on 31 March 1851, by which time he was 38 years old, Patrick was a "Farmer of 303 square acres employing 12 labourers"[6] and living in Ingliston just outside Edinburgh. On 23 January 1863, Patrick Gifford, still resident in Ingliston and still working as a farmer, married Barbara Sloan Grierson, a "farmer's daughter".[7] Barbara Grierson's "usual residence" is given as

---

[4]   Census of Scotland, 31 March 1851, the original document being "extracted from the Census Records" on 23 March 1861. According to the Census of Scotland, 31 March 1851, Patrick was 38 years old, which implies that he was born in 1813.

[5]   See footnote 6 below.

[6]   Census of Scotland, 31 March 1851.

[7]   Patrick Gifford's marriage certificate is dated 23 January 1863. According to this document Patrick Gifford's father, John Gifford, also a farmer, was already deceased.

Bishopton.[8] At the time of their marriage, according to their marriage certificate, Patrick was 50 years old while Barbara was 22. Barbara's father, John Barber Grierson, is recorded in the same document as also being a farmer.

Thomas Johnstone Carlyle Gifford was born on 14 January 1881. When he was born his father, Patrick, was 68 years old and his mother, Barbara, was 40. Carlyle was one of six children. He shined from an early age as a pupil and from 1896 to 1897 he attended George Watson's College, a well-known private school in Edinburgh. At Watson's he was awarded the 'Certificate of Merit for distinction in mathematics, Latin and Greek'. After school, Carlyle attended Edinburgh University where he played soccer for the university team. He went on to study law, serving his apprenticeship with Ward J. Cook, WS, before becoming private clerk to Sir Henry Cook. Sir Henry wrote a personal recommendation for Gifford on the basis of which Baillie invited him to become a partner.

Appointed as a partner in 1907 by Augustus Baillie, the new law firm of Baillie and Gifford, WS, was formed in the same year in Edinburgh. The story of his appointment is told by Carlyle Gifford:

"The terms of Partnership were simple, on a small piece of note paper written out by Lyon Mackenzie and the terms were that I should get a guarantee of £300 per annum and one-third of the profits. Thus started a Partnership which was always of unallied happiness throughout. In the second year Augustus altered the terms of the Partnership so that I would share in the profits equally".[9]

---

[8]   The only Bishopton currently existing in Scotland is on the Firth of Clyde, west of Glasgow.

[9]   Undated typed memo written by Carlyle Gifford, p.1. This document is one of only two documents written by Carlyle Gifford (apart from his published letters to his wife, Maud, written when he was in the United States during the Second World War) that to the author's knowledge have survived. The other document is a paper on economic conditions in the United States written after the war by Gifford after a visit to that country.

In the same year that he entered the partnership Carlyle Gifford got married. On 11 June 1907 he married Maud Oriel Riata Pearson, daughter of Charles Henry Pearson, a lawyer.

At that time, according to Gifford, there was only a "...small nucleus of business".[10] The firm employed only five clerks and of these only one was a qualified solicitor. The firm's main clients included Henry Trotter of Mortonhall and Charterhall, Augustus Baillie's brother-in-law; Jim Baillie of Dochfour, Augustus' brother; and from the Fletcher side of the earlier law partnership, the McGregor family.

Baillie and Gifford complemented each other well. Gifford was to a large extent left to run the office while Baillie sought to extend the firm's client base through his family and friends and through his hunting and other social activities. Baillie's membership of Edinburgh's New Club helped cement his business ties and Gifford also became a member. As Gifford recollects:

> "...the fact was that Augustus did not attempt to take any serious part in the detailed conduct of the business. He owned a house near Melrose and his primary wish was to hunt on Saturdays and Mondays and Wednesdays during the season. He was there in the office most of the other days and was invaluable if there was [sic] any general questions of policy to be considered. I would not wish to minimize the value that he was throughout the partnership to me, but it was not primarily as a lawyer".[11]

Gifford also acknowledged the importance of Baillie's social network in establishing the firm and expanding its business:

> "Another important factor in the development of the business was Augustus' friend Shelly Bontine, who had been at school with him and now owned a property in Argyllshire which we came to manage for him, particularly after war broke out. He came to live in Edinburgh holding a Commission of some kind up at the

---

[10] ibid, p.1.
[11] ibid, p.5.

Castle, but from our point of view his value was that he really acted as a standard bearer for us, and though I do not have direct evidence of that I am sure that from time to time he pushed, particularly at the New Club, the importance of this young firm of Baillie & Gifford, particularly in connection with an article which I wrote on inflation of credit and through his intimacy with Lord Tweeddale he was an important factor in the development of the Firm".[12]

However, Baillie and Gifford, WS, were soon to take their "...first step of progress"[13] when they became involved in the global rubber industry.

Baillie and Gifford's Involvement in the Rubber Industry: The Straits Mortgage and Trust Company, 1909

One of the tasks performed by Baillie and Gifford, WS, was to act as secretaries for private companies. Included amongst the firm's clients were the Aviemore Station Hotel Company (established with Baillie capital) and the Third Mile Rubber Company.[14] The latter would become of particular interest to the firm.

The reason was the close link between rubber and the motor car industry that had already launched the fourth global wave of technological and economic change. The industry had grown extremely rapidly from the time that it started as a viable commercial activity in 1895. In 1904 in the United States 22,800 cars were sold; by 1925 this would increase to 4 million annually. From 1909 to 1919 the growth rate of the industry reached a peak of 26% per annum. In 1907, the year that Baillie Gifford was established, there were approximately 250 car manufacturers in the US and more than 50 new manufacturers were entering annually.[15] The derived demand for rubber for car tyres had already created a boom for rubber (the rubber tree having been transplanted from its

---

[12] ibid, p.5.
[13] ibid, p.2.
[14] ibid, p.1.
[15] Klepper (1997), pp.152-4.

original habitat in the Amazon in Brazil to other locations such as Malaya and Ceylon).[16]

Baillie and Gifford's introduction to the opportunities for profitable investment in the rubber industry came through their connections with the McGregor family, originally introduced to Augustus Baillie by his partner, Fletcher.[17] 'Old Mr McGregor', as he was known to Carlyle Gifford, had three sons, two of whom were rubber planters in Malaya. In 1908, Alistair, the older brother, returned home to Edinburgh on leave. It was he who, in Gifford's words, "...made a valuable suggestion" to Augustus Baillie and Carlyle Gifford:

> "In 1907 one of the crises in American financial affairs occurred. Banks were closed for a time and generally a severe depression, which seriously affected the price and prospects of rubber planting companies. Up to then it had been customary in Malaya for managers, in addition to managing their company, to take up an area of land and develop it personally. In 1908 these men were in a difficulty because salaries had to be reduced and it was not easy for them to finance the land which they had taken up. Alistair McGregor suggested that a company be formed to lend such people on mortgage on their estates with a right of conversion into the equivalent of Ordinary Shares with the prospect of sharing in the future prosperity which seemed likely ultimately to return".[18]

It was this proposal that led to the establishment of the Straits Mortgage and Trust Company Limited, the prospectus for which was summarised in the *Glasgow Herald* on 20 March 1909. Regarding the purpose of the company, the prospectus stated that:

---

[16] For an account of the rubber industry and its booms and busts, see Newlands (1997).

[17] This account comes from the undated typed memo written by Carlyle Gifford.

[18] ibid, p.2.

"This Company has been formed for the purpose, inter alia, of lending money on the security of real estate in the Malay Peninsula, Ceylon, and elsewhere; more especially on the security of well-planted rubber estates, for the purpose of maintenance and development, until the tapping period is reached".

The prospectus went on to refer to the shortage of funds that created the possibility for profitable lending:

"During the last few years a large area of land, excellently suited for growing rubber, has been cleared and planted in the Malay Peninsular, Ceylon, and elsewhere. In addition to what the well-known Companies have done, much of this work has been carried out by private individuals, salaried managers of plantations, and others, and by private Companies. Many of these are known to be short of funds, having been led by a justifiable belief in the prospects of plantation rubber into planting operations which have left them with insufficient capital to keep their estates clean and in good order, and to pay costs of upkeep and management until the trees can be advantageously tapped.

"It is primarily to meet this demand for capital by granting loans upon such estates, on terms similar to those of convertible Debentures, that this Company has been formed.

"The terms of the loans will, in the majority of cases, include a right to the Company to convert its loan, or a part of it, at any time during a period of years into a share in the estate on which the loan is made, such share being arrived at by a comparison between the whole amount of the loan and the value of the estate when the loan is granted. Until this option of conversion is exercised (i.e. during the non-tapping period), the loan will carry a fixed rate of interest, and will be secured by a mortgage over the estate".

The prospectus goes on to reassure potential investors regarding the quality of the company's connections in the region of business:

> "Satisfactory arrangements have been made for the conduct of the Company's affairs in the Malay Peninsula, which is to be the first field of operations. The details of management there were fully discussed in December and January last with Mr J.A. MacGregor, the well-known Visiting Agent of the Anglo-Malay and other Rubber Companies, and with the senior partner of Messrs Allen & Gledhill, of Singapore, who were then in this country".[19]

At the first meeting of the directors of the Straits Mortgage and Trust Company Limited held on 18 March 1909 George Dunlop was appointed Chairman.[20] The Secretaries reported that 40,000 shares had been applied for. The "Directors accordingly allotted to each applicant the shares for which he had applied".[21] The Trust appointed the Royal Bank of Scotland and the Hong Kong and Shanghai Banking Corporation as its bankers. Baillie & Gifford, WS, of 12 Hill Street, Edinburgh, became the "solicitors and secretaries".

At the next meeting held on 30 March 1909 the directors "...considered the advisability of making preparations for doing Business in Ceylon".[22] Messrs Julius & Creasy, Solicitors, Ceylon were asked if they would act as the Company's agents in Ceylon. At the meeting held on 1 June 1909 the directors agreed that advertisements would be placed in the India Rubber journal, Ceylon Times, and the Straits Settlement Newspaper, indicating

---

[19] *Glasgow Herald*, 20 March 1909.

[20] 'Minute of Meeting of Directors of the Straits Mortgage and Trust Company Limited held on 18th March 1909', National Archives of Scotland, GD 378.4.1.

[21] ibid.

[22] 'Minute of Meeting of Directors of the Straits Mortgage and Trust Company Limited held on 30th March 1909', National Archives of Scotland, GD 378.4.1, p.11.

where the Straits Mortgage and Trust Company saw its major area of business.[23]

The details of the six directors are shown in Exhibit 3.1.

Exhibit 3.1. First directors of the Straits Mortgage and Trust Company Limited, 1909

Director	Credentials	Address
Augustus C. Baillie	Lieut.-Colonel, DSO, Director of Third Mile Rubber Company	Kirklands, Melrose
James S. Bontein	Chairman of Third Mile Rubber Company	Glencruittan, Oban.
George Dunlop	Writer to the Signet	20 Castle Street, Edinburgh
J. Maxtone Graham	Chartered Accountant	34 Charlotte Square, Edinburgh
J. Maclachlan of Maclachlan	Writer to the Signet, Director of the Sungei Kapar Rubber Company	48 Castle Street, Edinburgh
A.R. Wilson Wood	Managing Director of the Vallambrosa Rubber Company	7 Abbotsford Crescent, St Andrews

Source: *Glasgow Herald*, 20 March 1909.

However, it would be wrong to conclude that the early investments of the Straits Mortgage and Trust Company were only in Asia (largely Malaya and Ceylon). At the meeting of directors

---

[23] 'Minute of Meeting of Directors of the Straits Mortgage and Trust Company Limited held on 1st June 1909', National Archives of Scotland, GD 378.4.1.

held on 29 November 1910 reference was made to the purchase of 30 Union Pacific Railroad Company shares and to the sale of £1,000 of Mexico North Western Railway Bonds.[24] This shows that the Straits also made investments in America.

As Carlyle Gifford noted, the directors were largely friends of Augustus Baillie. Both James Maxtone Graham and John Maclachlan were, like Baillie, Members of the King's Bodyguard for Scotland (The Royal Company of Archers).[25] In fact all of the directors became significant shareholders in the Straits Mortgage and Trust Company. Although not a director, Carlyle Gifford, who attended the directors' meetings, was also a substantial shareholder. The first surviving list of shareholders provides information on those owning shares on 2 June 1915. Exhibit 3.2 shows the shareholdings by the Straits directors and also for Carlyle Gifford on this date.

Several important observations emerge from Exhibit 3.2. The first is the significant shareholdings by the Straits directors, who were amongst the company's largest shareholders. Clearly, the Straits company was set up to serve their own interests as well as those of their other shareholders. Secondly, the relatively large shareholding of Carlyle Gifford, who was not a director, reveals the influence that he must have wielded, not only in Baillie and Gifford, WS, but also in the Straits company itself and amongst its directors. Not only was Gifford (in 1915) the seventh largest shareholder, his shareholdings were larger than three of the six directors, including George Dunlop, the chairman. While Gifford held 2,560 shares, Dunlop held 2,000. Baillie held the relatively small number of 1,690.

Further analysis of the list of shareholders provides more details on the savings pool that the Straits company tapped in order to make its overseas investments. Some of this information is provided in Exhibit 3.3.

Several observations may be made on the basis of Exhibit 3.3 (which, it should be stressed, provides data only for the largest

---

[24] 'Minute of Meeting of Directors of the Straits Mortgage and Trust Company Limited held on 29 November 1910', National Archives of Scotland, GD 378.4.1, p.144.

[25] *Scottish Biographies*. (1938). Glasgow: Jackson, Son and Co.

shareholders, that is for those owning 500 or more shares on 2 June 1915, the first date for which shareholder information is available). The first observation is that most of these shareholders came from Scotland. Scottish shareholders held 75% of all the shares held by shareholders owning 500 or more shares. They constituted 72.5% of the total number of larger shareholders.

Exhibit 3.2. Shareholding by directors of the Straits Mortgage and Trust Company Limited, 1915

Director	Shareholding	Ranking
Augustus C. Baillie	1,690	15th largest shareholder
James S. Bontein	5,810	1st largest shareholder
George Dunlop	2,000	8th largest shareholder
J. Maxtone Graham	1,540	16th largest shareholder[1]
J. Maclachlan of Maclachlan	4,302	2nd largest shareholder
A.R. Wilson Wood	2,711	6th largest shareholder
[Carlyle Gifford] (not a director)	[2,560]	7th largest shareholder

[1] Joint shareholding with John L. Mounsey, 34 Charlotte Square, Edinburgh.
Source: Shareholders in the Shareholder Register, The Straits Mortgage and Trust Company Limited, on 2 June 1915, National Archives of Scotland.

Exhibit 3.3. Geographical location of largest shareholders in the Straits Mortgage and Trust Company Limited, 1915 (holding 500 or more shares)

Location	Number of shareholders	Proportion of shares held [1] (%)	Proportion of total number of shareholders (%)
Edinburgh	29	37.0	36.25
Glasgow	3	2.0	3.75
Perth	1	1.0	1.25
Dundee	5	4.5	6.25
Other Scotland	20	30.5	25.00
Total Scotland	**58**	**75.0**	**72.5**
London	13	18.5	16.25
Other England	8	5.5	10.00
Total England	**21**	**24.0**	**26.25**
Foreign	1	1.0	1.25
GRAND TOTAL	**80**	**100**	**100**

[1] i.e. proportion of total number of shares held by shareholders with 500 or more shares.
Source: Shareholders in the Shareholder Register, The Straits Mortgage and Trust Company Limited, on 2 June 1915, National Archives of Scotland.

Secondly, not surprisingly most of the larger shareholders came from Edinburgh. Edinburgh residents held 37% of the shares and made up 36% of the larger shareholders. Thirdly, the saving pool that the Straits company tapped did not extend much to other Scottish cities. Significantly, Glasgow residents only owned 2% of the shares and were only 3.75% of the larger shareholders. The figures are much the same for Perth and Dundee, although Dundonians owned a larger proportion of the shares and were a larger proportion of the shareholders, than their Glaswegian counterparts. However, the figure for 'other' Scottish share-holders is rather substantial, accounting for a greater proportion of shares and shareholders than Glasgow, Perth and Dundee combined. 'Other Scotland' controlled 30.5% of the shares and constituted 25% of the number of larger shareholders. This reflected the Straits company's constituency amongst Scottish landed social groups.

Fourthly, and again not surprisingly, is the substantial holding by Londoners even though collectively they are outweighed by 'other Scotland'. Londoners owned 18.5% of these shares and were 16.25% of the larger shareholders. Finally, non-UK residents owned only 1% of the shares and were 1.25% of the larger shareholders.

Several other observations may be added. The great majority of shareholders were private investors. Very few companies were share-holders. In descending order, there were only the following three companies included amongst those holding 500 or more shares (their number of shares in brackets): Commercial Bank of Scotland Ltd. (1,120); Union Trustee Company of Australia (1,000); and Scottish Canadian Trust Ltd (500).

The vast majority of shareholders were from the legal profession, including Writers to the Signet (11 shareholders), Justices of the Peace (2) and Advocates (2). There were also many accountants (5) and quite a few shareholders with military titles (7). Other categories included: Gentleman (7, the definition of which is unclear); Baron (1, Rt Hon Sydney Herbert, 3,000 shares); Baronet (1, Sir John A. Dewar MP, 1,000 shares); Lord (1, Henry F.M.D Scott, 500 shares); Merchant (2); Rubber Industry (2); Farmer (2); Woollen Manufacturer (1); Landed Proprietor (1); Brewer (2, William and Harry Younger); and Banker (1). There were 10 women (who were recorded separately under titles such as Mrs, Miss, Widow and Spinster). This is shown in Exhibit 3.4.

Exhibit 3.4. Listed occupation of shareholders in the Straits Mortgage and Trust Company, 2 June 1915

Listed occupation	Number of shareholders with 500 or more shares
Writers to the Signet	11
'Women' (who were recorded separately under titles such as Mrs, Miss, Widow, and Spinster)	10
'Military Titles '	7
Gentleman (the definition of which is unclear)	7
Accountant	5
Advocate	2
Brewer	2
Farmer	2
Justice of the Peace	2
Merchant	2
'Rubber Industry'	2
Banker	1
Baron	1
Baronet	1
Landed Proprietor	1
Lord	1
Woollen Manufacturer	1

Source: Shareholders in the Shareholder Register, The Straits Mortgage and Trust Company Limited, on 2 June 1915, National Archives of Scotland.

Unfortunately, however, the venture did not turn out as successfully as had been hoped. Carlyle Gifford explains:

"An issue of capital was made but was not very successful only £70,000 being subscribed. This took place in 1909 and by that time circumstances had improved in the United States, and with the development of the motor car industry there was a keen demand for rubber so the price rose to 10 [shillings] a pound and over. In these circumstances the individual planters had no difficulty in raising money so that it was not easy for the new Company to invest the money which had been subscribed".[26]

Nevertheless, all was not lost as a result of the reasonable investments that were in the event made. The Straits:

"...did however lend £20,000 to the Vidor Company with a right of conversion at 22/6d. [22 shillings and 6 pence] and this proved very profitable because in due course we were able to convert the debenture and sell the resulting shares at over 40/- a share. The bulk of the remainder of the money had been invested in a Debenture, also convertible, on the Dalkeith Rubber Company of Ceylon. It was soon found however that that estate was by no means a first class one and the prospect of converting our Debenture was poor. However, the Debenture was repayable in...1916 or 1917, and by that time the Chancellor of the Exchequer was issuing Treasury Bills at 6%. The result was that on getting back our money terms for re-investment were very favourable, and the Company began to prosper. That is the origin of the Company".[27]

---

[26] Undated typed memo written by Carlyle Gifford, p.2.

[27] ibid, pp.2-3.

Change in Name of the Straits Company to the Scottish Mortgage and Trust Company

At the fourth annual general meeting of the shareholders in the Straits Mortgage and Trust Company Limited, held on 6 May 1913 with George Dunlop chairing, the decision was taken to change the name of the company to the Scottish Mortgage and Trust Company. The Chairman gave the reasons for the proposal: "When the company was started four years ago its object was to lend money on the security of real estate, more especially on the security of well-planted rubber estates".[28] However, the intentions of the company had been frustrated: "In consequence of the great boom in rubber planting which took place shortly after the inception of the company [i.e. Straits], owners of plantations were able to obtain capital on very easy terms indeed, so that the door was rather closed against us in that direction".[29]

It was therefore decided by the directors that the Straits company should be transformed into an "ordinary investment company" and its name be altered accordingly: "I intimated on a previous occasion that we might, as we have already done, decide to exercise the powers conferred upon us by carrying on the business of an ordinary investment company, and that is what we suggest doing in the future. We have therefore thought that as the original name of the company was fixed upon in expectation of doing more business in connection with rubber plantations, we had better, seeing that we were no longer working in that connection, adopt some other name that might perhaps commend itself more to the general public. We have accordingly chosen the name of 'The Scottish Mortgage and Trust Company'…".[30]

[In passing, it is worth noting the record of an interchange reported in *The Economist* between a shareholder in the Straits company, a Mr W.C. Findlay, and the chairman, Mr George Dunlop, that took place during the discussion at this fourth annual

---

[28]   Chairman George Dunlop's speech to the fourth annual general meeting of the shareholders in the Straits Mortgage and Trust Company Limited, held on 6 May 1913 at 12 Hill Street, Edinburgh, quoted in *The Economist*, 10 May 1913, pp.1104-5.

[29]   *The Economist*, 10 May 1913, p.1104.

[30]   ibid, p.1104.

general meeting. The questions and answers give something of the flavour of the relationship which existed at the time between investment company directors and their shareholders:

> **"A Shareholder's Enquiry**
> The Chairman, having invited questions,
> Mr W.C. Findlay said that he gathered from the chairman's remarks that the company was no longer interested in rubber plantations.
> The Chairman: Not to the large extent we expected to be.
> Mr W.C. Findlay, continuing, said he would just like to say that, speaking from the shareholders' point of view, they were rather in the dark as to what they [i.e. the Straits company] really were in. He thought it would be interesting to know. They trusted the directors, and expected the directors to trust them.
> The Chairman said that the secretaries would be pleased to show the questioner a list of the investments at the close of the meeting. They had rather followed the example of two other companies he was interested in, and had not published a list of their investments, but, as he had stated, they would be pleased to show them to any shareholder after the meeting".[31]]

CONSOLIDATION AND EXPANSION: BAILLIE GIFFORD, 1914-1945

3 Glenfinlas Street

In 1913, Baillie and Gifford, WS, purchased 3 Glenfinlas Street, Edinburgh (the capital put up by Augustus Baillie), and the firm moved to this address.[32]

---

[31] *The Economist*, 10 May 1913, pp.1104.
[32] Undated typed memo written by Carlyle Gifford.

New Investment Trusts

The Scottish Mortgage and Trust Company

By 1912, only five years after Baillie and Gifford formed their partnership, the firm had established itself as a credible manager of other people's (and the partners' own) investments. They had successfully entered a new market (the market for investment trusts) and the knowledge that they had accumulated about the workings of this market and about how to establish and manage investment trusts provided them with a solid base for future expansion.

In 1914, Baillie and Gifford's second investment trust, the Edinburgh, Dundee and Aberdeen Investment Co., was established, as is shown in Exhibit 3.5. The Scottish Canadian Mortgage Co. Ltd. was established in 1912 and its management was transferred to Baillie Gifford in 1918.

Between 1909 and 1927, as is also shown in Exhibit 3.5, Baillie and Gifford established a total of five investment trusts. This put the firm in a strong position to expand further.

Monks Investment Trust: origin of the 'ecclesiasticals'

The fundamental soundness of Baillie Gifford is apparent from the advantage the firm was able to take from the misfortunes of others. In the late 1920s, three new investment trusts were established by a merchant bank[33] in London. The first, established in 1927, was named the Friars Investment Trust (because the investment trust was established in Austin Friars in London). In the following two years two further investment trusts were set up, Abbots in 1928 and Monks in 1929 – collectively known informally as the 'ecclesiasticals'. Exhibit 3.6 provides the details.

---

[33] The name of this merchant bank is not known. (Interview with Richard Burns.)

Exhibit 3.5. History of the six investment trusts
established by Baillie Gifford, 1909-1927

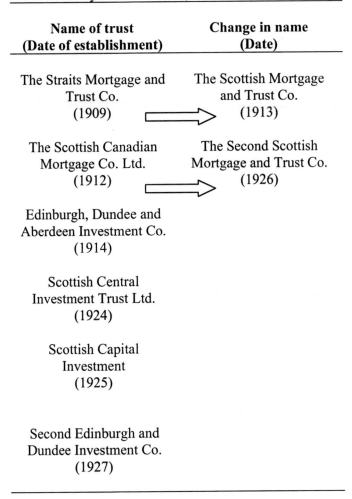

Name of trust (Date of establishment)	Change in name (Date)
The Straits Mortgage and Trust Co. (1909)	The Scottish Mortgage and Trust Co. (1913)
The Scottish Canadian Mortgage Co. Ltd. (1912)	The Second Scottish Mortgage and Trust Co. (1926)
Edinburgh, Dundee and Aberdeen Investment Co. (1914)	
Scottish Central Investment Trust Ltd. (1924)	
Scottish Capital Investment (1925)	
Second Edinburgh and Dundee Investment Co. (1927)	

Exhibit 3.6. History of the 'ecclesiasticals'

Name of trust (Date, place of establishment)	Takeover of management by Baillie Gifford	Merger (Date)
Friars Investment Trust (1927, London)	1931	Monks Investment Trust (1969)
Abbots Investment Trust (1928, London)	1931	Monks Investment Trust (1969)
Monks Investment Trust (1929, London)	1931	Monks Investment Trust (1969)

As a result of the fallout that followed the 'Great Crash' in 1929 the merchant bank collapsed and Baillie and Gifford were invited to take over the management of the three 'ecclesiasticals'. The decision regarding the Friars Investment Trust was made at the board meeting held at 13/14 Austin Friars, EC2, on Thursday, 11 June 1931. In the chair was Sir Auckland C. Geddes (an acquaintance of Carlyle Gifford) and also present were the other directors, Sir George Jessel, J.N. Buchanan and A.R. Cook. The minutes of the meeting record that:

> "The meeting having considered the arrangements to be made for the future management of the Company, and having been informed that Messrs Baillie Gifford and Company of 3 Glenfinlas Street, Edinburgh, who are about to open an office in London, are willing to accept appointment as Managers and Secretaries...from 30th June 1931".[34]

---

[34] Minutes of Board Meeting held at 13/14 Austin Friars, EC2, on Thursday, 11 June 1931. (National Archives of Scotland, GD 378/1/4, pp.85-6.)

Two conditions were stipulated. The first was a general provision relating to duties and Baillie Gifford's costs:

"Messrs Baillie, Gifford & Company shall perform the normal duties of Managers and Secretaries of an Investment Trust Company and shall provide office accommodation and staff at their own expense, their employment to continue during the pleasure of the Directors, subject to reasonable notice on either side".[35]

The second related to remuneration:

"The remuneration of the Managers and Secretaries is to be arrived at in the following way:-
Out of the sum provided by the Articles of Association to be set aside to cover expenses of management there shall first be paid such charges as Stationery, Bank Charges [etc]...which are to be met thereout according to the Articles, and thereafter the balance remaining in each year shall be divided between the Directors on the one side and the Managers and Secretaries on the other in the proportions of sixty per cent to the Directors and forty per cent to the Managers and Secretaries. The Managers and Secretaries shall be entitled to retain any commissions paid to them as Agents according to the rules of the Stock Exchange, or in respect of placing or other commissions paid by issuing houses or others on the understanding that they are not to be passed on to clients. It is understood that the Managers and Secretaries will arrange that the brokerage to be paid by the Company shall in all cases be the lowest possible, and in particular the Company shall have the advantage of the reduced rate of brokerage

---

[35] Minutes of Board Meeting held at 13/14 Austin Friars, EC2, on Thursday, 11 June 1931. (National Archives of Scotland, GD 378/1/4, p.86.)

which is allowable by brokers on certain transactions and which is not divisible by them".[36]

Two years earlier, in the minutes for 1929, it was stated that directors had received the following Directors' Fees: for Messrs Balfour,[37] Buchanan, Cook and Jessel, £422; for Sir E.C. Geddes, who was Chairman, £622.[38]

In 1932 the geographical distribution of the investments of the Friars Trust were as shown in Exhibit 3.7.

Exhibit 3.7. Geographical distribution of investments of the Friars Investment Trust, 1932[39]

Region	Proportion
UK	23.52%
America (excluding US and Canada)	14.82%
USA	14.19%
Asia	5.70%

The total capital of the three 'ecclesiastical' investment trusts at their establishment was £1.6 million. By 1979 (by which time they had merged under the name of Monks) the total value of their net assets had increased to £69 million: "A substantial proportion of their funds was invested in the US by Baillie Gifford".[40]

---

[36] Minutes of Board Meeting held at 13/14 Austin Friars, EC2, on Thursday, 11 June 1931 (underlining in original). (National Archives of Scotland, GD 378/1/4, p.86.)

[37] In the minutes for 1941 he is referred to as "The Hon. J.M. Balfour".

[38] National Archives of Scotland, GD 378/1/4, p.24.

[39] ibid, p.10.

[40] National Archives of Scotland, GD 378.

Baillie Gifford's Investment Trusts, 1964

The market value of Baillie Gifford's investment trusts in 1964 is shown in Exhibit 3.8 (which also includes the investment trusts of Ivory and Sime and Martin Currie).

The Independent Investment Company

By the early 1920s, Carlyle Gifford had greatly extended his experience, knowledge and reputation as an investment manager. One notable indication of his standing was his creation, with John Maynard Keynes and Oswald T. Falk (Keynes' London stockbroker), of the Independent Investment Company on 8 January 1924. The company's prospectus states that its aim was to take advantage of the "periodic credit cycle" during which changes in the relative price of various assets open up important investment opportunities. However, the trust's performance was very poor. Nevertheless, although the company did not perform particularly well and was soon wound up, the endeavour revealed Gifford to be a player of note in the UK investment management world and benefited the standing of Baillie and Gifford, WS.

Investment Trust Directorships: Carlyle Gifford and Augustus Baillie

By the early 1930s, Carlyle Gifford was director of 13 companies, most of which were investment companies and trusts. By this time, "...he was just as likely to be a member of a fund managed by another house, as of one managed by Baillie and Gifford, WS".[41] Indeed, the 'Edinburgh network' of fund managers was a rather tightly-knit group and its members were bound together by numerous formal and informal links. Some of the investment trusts in which Carlyle Gifford was a director are shown in Exhibit 3.9.

---

[41]   Slaven and Checkland (1990), p.406.

Exhibit 3.8. Baillie Gifford's investment trusts, 1964. (Market value of investments, 1964, £000)

Name of Group	Name of Trusts	Market Value of Investments (1964)
	Edinburgh and Dundee Investment Co.	18,415
	Second Edinburgh and Dundee Investment Co.	8,488
	Scottish Capital Investment Co.	12,860
	Scottish Central Investment Trust	13,101
Baillie, Gifford		
	Scottish Mortgage and Trust	28,775
	Second Scottish Mortgage and Trust	10,328
	Abbots Investment Trust	8,876
	Friars Investment Trust	9,763
	Monks Investment Trust	8,324
	Winterbottom Trust [1]	6,364
	Total	**125,494**
	Atlantic Assets Trust	5,221
Ivory and Sime	British Assets Trust	42,149
	Second British Assets Trust	13,906
	Total	**61,376**
	Canadian and Foreign Investment Trust	4,449
	Scottish Eastern Investment Trust	21,161
Martin Currie	Scottish Ontario Investment Trust	8,697
	Scottish American Mortgage Co. (from 19/3/1966)	14,898
	Western Canada Investment Co.	1,297
	Total	**50,502**

[1] The Winterbottom Trust was a trust set up by the Winterbottom Book Cloth company, the management of which was taken over by Baillie Gifford in 1935. [42]
Source: Burton and Corner (1968), pp.351-3.

---

[42]   Interview with Richard Burns.

Exhibit 3.9. Some investment trusts in which Carlyle Gifford was a director

Name of Trust	Date Established	Managers
Scottish Investment Trust Co. Ltd.	1887	
Second Scottish Investment Trust Co. Ltd.	1889	
United States Trust Company of Scotland Ltd.	1884	R.G. Simpson, CA
General Scottish Trust Ltd.	1914	
Investors' Mortgage Security Co. Ltd.	1891	Shepherd and Wedderburn, WS
Scottish and Canadian General Investment Co. Ltd.	1910	Maxtone, Graham and Sime, CA
Second Investors' Mortgage Security Co. Ltd.	1914	
Melville Trust Ltd.	1929	Scott-Moncrieff, Thomson and Shiells, CA
Scottish Capital Investment Co. Ltd.	1925	Baillie, Gifford and Co.
Scottish Central Investment Trust Ltd.	1924	

Source: Glasgow, G. (1932) *The Scottish Investment Trust Companies* and Slaven and Checkland (1990), p.406.

Amongst the non-investment trust companies for which Carlyle Gifford was chairman were the Vallambrosa Rubber Company, the Scottish Widows' Fund and The Scottish Tea and Lands Co. of Ceylon, Limited.[43]

Augustus Baillie tended to be on the board of directors only of investment trusts managed by Baillie Gifford. These trusts are shown in Exhibit 3.10.

Exhibit 3.10. Investment trusts in which Augustus Baillie was a director

Name of Trust	Date Established	Managers
Edinburgh and Dundee Investment Co. Ltd.	1914	Baillie, Gifford and Co.
Scottish Mortgage and Trust Co. Ltd.	1909	Baillie, Gifford and Co.
Second Scottish Mortgage and Trust Co. Ltd. (formerly Scottish Canadian)	1912	Baillie, Gifford and Co.
Second Edinburgh and Dundee Investment Co. Ltd.	1927	Baillie, Gifford and Co.

Source: Glasgow, G. (1932) *The Scottish Investment Trust Companies.*

---

[43] Meeting of the 35th Ordinary General Meeting of the Vallambrosa Rubber Company, Edinburgh, Chairman, T.J.C. Gifford, reported in *The Times*, 14 July 1939; 130th Stated Annual Meeting of the Scottish Widows' Fund and Life Assurance Society, Edinburgh, Chairman of the Ordinary Court of Directors, T.J.C. Gifford, reported in *The Times*, 19 April 1944; reported in *The Times*, 9 December, 1927.

Baillie, Gifford and Co. and Biggart, Baillie and Gifford, WS: Separation of the Investment Management Firm from the Law Firm

In 1927, Baillie, Gifford and Co. was created to deal with investment management and was separated from Baillie and Gifford, WS (the law firm). [In 1974 Baillie & Gifford, WS, merged with Biggart Lumsden & Co of Glasgow, the descendant of Weir and Biggart, established as a law firm in 1894, to become Biggart Baillie & Gifford W.S. with offices in Edinburgh and Glasgow. Sir Thomas Biggart worked closely with employers' organisations in Glasgow including those in the shipbuilding and engineering industries.]

The reason for the separation was that Carlyle Gifford wanted to make some of the people that he had appointed on the investment side of the business partners. However, since they were not qualified lawyers this was not possible. Separation of the two businesses provided a solution to this problem. Those who were made partners of Baillie Gifford and Co were William Watson and Alan Brown (who are referred to later).

Carlyle Gifford Serves Britain in the US during the Second World War

On 27 September 1939 Carlyle Gifford received a letter from Montagu Norman, Governor of the Bank of England, inviting him to join a committee to advise the Treasury on the acquisition and sale of foreign securities in aid of the war effort. Walter Wingham, a member of the committee and director of the Bank, was asked to go to the US to examine the situation there. He invited Gifford to go with him.

After they returned to London in December 1939 it was intended that Wingham would go back to the US alone to take charge of the requisitioning and realisation of UK-owned dollar securities. Due to the illness of his wife, however, Wingham could not return to the US and the Bank asked Gifford to do the job. On 17 January 1940 he went to the US. After a brief holiday back in Edinburgh in September he returned to the US at the beginning of October 1940, finally coming back to the UK in August 1941.

Whilst in the US, Gifford wrote regular letters to his wife, Maud, whom he had married on 11 June 1907. These letters were published in book form in 1969 by an Edinburgh publisher.[44] The aim in this section is to review this book with a view to understanding what light, if any, the book throws on Carlyle Gifford, the man and his life.

As the reader quickly discovers, the book is rather curious in that its purposes are unclear. The foreword to the book is little more than half a page and essentially says little more than what is contained in the first paragraph of this section. It is only on page 80 (in a book of 143 pages) that, in a letter dated 20 February 1941, Gifford says to Maud, "...this has been a very long story.... But I wanted you to have it all and to record it perhaps to look back on in time to come".

One of his purposes, it seems, is to produce a detailed record of his time in the US. And the record is certainly very detailed, focusing mainly on the people that he meets, both during the course of his official business dealings as well as socially. His blow-by-blow account of his activities is not without interest, principally because Gifford was able to meet many of the 'high and mighty' in the financial and related political worlds in New York and Washington at this crucial historical juncture just before the US entered the war on the Allied side.

Perhaps the best summary of Gifford's business in the US, and the way he was perceived in America, is given in an article in *Time* published on 4 March 1940 titled 'Scot in Wall Street'. The article begins by explaining the significance of Gifford's mission from the point of view of the US:

"A Damoclean dagger rather than sword are the £1,420,000,000 worth of U.S. stocks and bonds held by Allied investors. Their value is less than 2% of that of all securities listed on the New York Stock Exchange. But under the imminent and certain threat of World War II, the hair that held this dagger over U.S. securities markets looked scarily tenuous to market men. If French and British investors had sold their holdings in a panicky rush

---

[44] Gifford, T.J.C. 1969. *Letters from America*. Edinburgh: T. & A. Constable.

for dollars, the dagger would have dropped on an already queasy market, drawn real blood".[45]

The threat to US securities markets, however, was reduced by the decision taken by the British government to control the sale of British-owned US securities. It was Carlyle Gifford's job to ensure that the sale of these assets in the US, necessary to help finance the war, went smoothly in the national interest. This promised to minimise the resulting instability in US financial markets. *Time* suggests that Gifford's experience and reputation added further to a sense of confidence:

"So it was that the market breathed easier in late August [1939] when Britain forced its nationals (holders of better than half of the Allied hoard) to register their U.S. securities, sell then only with Government permission. Last week it breathed still more freely when Britain announced that Scot Securities Tycoon, T.J. Carlyle Gifford was in Manhattan to handle the orderly liquidation of British holdings".[46]

One imagines that Gifford might have been slightly embarrassed at being referred to publicly as a 'tycoon', although he probably took some satisfaction at the itemisation of some of his credentials. Not only might this strengthen his hand in the forthcoming bargaining process involved in the sale of the British assets, it might also increase his personal credibility:

"No nervous Nellie to be panicked into witless sales is tweedy fifty-ish Scot Gifford, Edinburgh solicitor, chairman of eight British Investment Trusts, director of 22 British companies. Nor will he be a sucker for casual Wall Street advice. Twenty-five percent of the investment portfolios of many British Investment Trusts is in U.S.

---

[45] ibid, p.23.
[46] ibid, p.23.

securities, and Scot Gifford has long known his way around the Street as well as around the City".[47]

Time then went on to explain the general details of the deal and the benefits to the British side:

"To stock their man's first showcase, the British Government requisitioned outright all British holdings in 60 U.S. stocks. To His Majesty's subjects His Majesty's Government will pay the market price of their securities as of Feb. 17 in sterling. As Scot Gifford sells them here, the British Government will pocket its dollars for future U.S. material purchases, will thus have added to its present hoard of £2,600,000,000 in liquid gold and dollars".[48]

Gifford may also not have been unhappy at the very American way in which the source of his power in the US was made explicit:

"On Solicitor Gifford's first list were equities in plenty of profitable U.S. industries – Du Pont, Douglas Aircraft, American Tobacco, Santa Fe, Norfolk & Western, Colgate-Palmolive Peet.... Last week many a hungry broker hoped he would be tapped for help, get a fat commission in their sale. But who would be tapped, what commission would be paid, how rapidly the first block of equities would be sold, few in Wall Street knew, if any knew at all. Mr Gifford was as hard to find as a sliced brassie shot on a Scottish moor. In Manhattan for a month before his appointment was announced, he had been seen by partners of J.P. Morgan & Co., few others".[49]

Little wonder, then, that Carlyle Gifford was in much demand, wined and dined by the high and the mighty. Apart from J.P. Morgan & Co – which for some reason immediately became the

---

[47] ibid, pp.23-4.
[48] ibid, p.24.
[49] ibid, p.24.

main adviser to Gifford and the British side, a role that Gifford's letters make clear officials attempted to keep discreet – most of the top Wall Street firms and their most senior people went out of their way to court Gifford. He was invited not only to their offices but also to their sumptuous homes, both in the city and their weekend country residences.

For his part, Gifford seems to have responded well to all the attention, and on the whole greatly enjoyed his interactions with his new acquaintances. He was impressed with the relative absence of 'class distinctions' in the US, commenting in one letter that two of the people he had met "…would have had peerages in [Great Britain] and I doubt if the next generation could then have been as simple and un-removed from other Americans as they are to-day. Americans are undoubtedly right when they talk of the [absence of] class distinctions in [the] USA as compared with [Great Britain]".[50] In places his criticisms of this aspect of British society at the time emerge, such as his comment about one British visitor to the US who he thought "…belongs quite too much to an outworn world of aristocracy and privilege".[51]

However, this did not mean that Gifford was un-ambivalent about the Americans. In one of his letters, for example, he recounted an incident when the British colleague with him "spoilt" a social occasion "…by thanking the Americans very fulsomely for their help and asking them to buy autographs to help the Red Cross". His reflections on his own feelings in this situation reveal not only his ambivalence but at the same time a degree of self-insight: "I felt it was humiliating. For I share your [i.e. Maud's] feelings about the Americans. But sometimes I wonder if I am unjust to them and if any annoyance with them is not partly due to envy and jealousy, and then that my contempt for them may be just a protective covering to save me from having to admit to myself that [these] two feelings come into it".[52]

However, the letters also reflect another side to Gifford, the side that typically emerged when he loosened his tie after a day of intense interactions – business or social – and returned to the

---

[50] ibid, p.49.
[51] ibid, p.127.
[52] ibid, p.121.

solitude of his room. This is the more vulnerable Carlyle Gifford who, not surprisingly, also had to deal with his emotions that of necessity had been held in check by the intensity. It was at times such as these that Gifford expressed how much he missed Maud and how nostalgic he was for Edinburgh and their Scottish country home, Pogbie.

Indeed, in his fifth letter, written on 26 January 1940, only nine days after he had set sail for New York, he confesses to Maud that "I don't think I am so 'down' by any means as I was last time [i.e. on his first official trip to the US during November and December 1939], but yet I have a horrid gnawing ache for home and a probably long stretch ahead looks rather awful! But it can't be avoided and I can see nothing to be done about it. One must buoy oneself up with thoughts of the work one is doing.... I feel your loving care behind me".[53]

In his next letter, written three days later on 29 January 1940, he reports that "...this afternoon I am going to see an apartment at the Hampshire House. I am afraid it may be very expensive but it is important to have pleasant surroundings. I find the mornings so trying and also a little the last hour before going to bed. I expect it is the lack of all the foolish little nothings of gossip, telephonings, one's own books, etc. which fill up the time and one's mind at home. Without them the longing and ache for home – particularly, I suppose, in war time – are very trying". More optimistically, however, he acknowledges that "The rest of the time is often delightful".[54] These understandable sentiments are expressed at regular intervals throughout the book.

More surprising, however, are the absences in the letters. For example, there is nothing about Baillie Gifford & Co and the colleagues he left in charge of the firm. And although he is meticulous in recording his own activities and reactions there is very little about his own family. Whilst his son Charles is referred to occasionally – and at one point he talks about the possibility of Charles joining him in the US[55] – the references are impersonal. Furthermore, there is very little about Maud, about her response to

---

[53] ibid, p.10.
[54] ibid, pp.10-11.
[55] ibid, p.20.

his absence and about the vicissitudes of her life in war-bound Edinburgh.

One of the few exceptions comes towards the end of the book when, in a letter dated 5 July 1941 (he returned to London in August 1941), Gifford tries to allay Maud's worries about their son Charles who was at that time a British attaché in Russia. He also adds, "I am sorry about the deafness and thinness, dear one. Do what you can about the latter", but in the following sentence continues, "I don't feel as sure as you are about my looks. I think I am becoming much more lined. However, that can't be helped and I am very fit. I am looking forward very much now to coming home. I think I find the weekends trying, as I am cut off from compatriots...".[56]

Disappointingly, we learn next to nothing about Gifford's background (there are, surprisingly, almost no memories, recollections or associations relating to his earlier history). The only exception comes in his record of a dinner held in his honour when he responded to a toast to his health and "...told of my father's operations in American Rails in the '70s [i.e. 1870s], of the American atmosphere – visitors and Harpers Young People – in which I was brought up, our attempt to go to N.Y. [New York] in 1907...".[57] Perhaps it was no coincidence that in Gifford's view this short talk, which essentially contained a discreet patriotic plea for American assistance in the war effort, "...went extremely well, probably the best thing I have done apart from argument in a Court".[58] Unfortunately, we still know very little about Carlyle Gifford's background and earlier life.

---

[56] ibid, p.128.
[57] Letter dated 16 April 1940. 1907 was the year that Gifford joined Augustus Baillie in forming the legal partnership, Baillie and Gifford, WS. ibid, p.31.
[58] ibid, p.31.

CHAPTER

4

BAILLIE GIFFORD – 1945 TO THE PRESENT

1945-1976: CONSERVATIVE BUT SUCCESSFUL PROGRESS

1945-1950

Carlyle Gifford's return to Scotland

Having completed his duties in the United States, Carlyle Gifford returned to the United Kingdom in August 1941. One imagines that he returned with some apprehension. In the letter written in the US on 5 July 1941 to his wife Maud, Gifford confessed, "I am looking forward very much now to coming home. I think I find the weekends trying, as I am cut off from compatriots and I look forward to them now with quite a little anxiety".[1]

There were several reasons for Gifford's anxiety. To begin with, in his absence Baillie Gifford had been run by William Watson who had become a partner in Baillie, Gifford & Co before the war. As Gifford's US diary (written in the form of regular letters to Maud) makes clear, his attention was totally consumed by his duties in the United States, including his hectic social activities. The affairs of Baillie Gifford were doubtless far from his mind. Indeed, there is no reference at all in his entire diary to Baillie Gifford and its employees.

However, by July 1941, with his US negotiations almost completed, Gifford must have begun turning at least some of his thoughts to his business in Edinburgh. As a man used to being in the driving seat, a proclivity if anything reinforced by his experiences in the US that gave him direct and personal contact

---

[1] Gifford (1969), p.128.

with some of the most powerful people in the US financial community, Gifford must have realised that tensions would inevitably be raised by his return to Baillie Gifford. Hence his feelings of anxiety are understandable. It is natural that William Watson would have reciprocated these feelings. In the absence of the controlling and demanding Gifford, Watson no doubt enjoyed his independence. But both men must have been concerned at the prospect of the resumption of their business and personal relationship.

The organisational hierarchy in Baillie Gifford

There is, unfortunately, no record of what transpired in Baillie Gifford on Carlyle Gifford's return and in the following few years. However, we do know that in the late 1940s, presumably after some degree of conflict with Gifford, Watson made the decision to leave Baillie Gifford to become the equivalent of the General Manager of the Bank of Scotland (later becoming Sir William Watson). Alan Brown, who like Watson had become a partner before the war, left and subsequently became manager of the Alliance Trust in Dundee, although thereafter he maintained cordial relations with Gifford. However, Ian Milne, in charge of accounting and administration, remained.

The departure of senior staff caused a crisis in Baillie Gifford. In order to try and resolve this crisis a meeting was held in Carlyle Gifford's Edinburgh apartment in order to decide whether it was necessary to recruit new senior staff. The outcome of this meeting was that further recruitment was not necessary (although it is not clear who attended this meeting and what their individual views were).

Equally importantly, this meeting also resulted in *de facto* agreement regarding the new chain of command in Baillie Gifford. Carlyle Gifford, who at this time was about 66 years old and was the sole owner of Baillie Gifford & Co, remained the effective chairman of the company. However, George Chiene became, in effect, the senior partner in day-to-day charge of the firm (a sort of chief operating officer) with Ernest Dawson the next most senior. Ian Milne was persuaded to move from administration to investment and the administrative duties were passed to Bill

Clunie. However, Ian Milne was not very happy with having to make decisions and being answerable to Carlyle Gifford and took early retirement in the late 1950's.

George Chiene

George Turcan Chiene was born on 15 November 1907 (the same year that Baillie and Gifford, WS, was formed). He was the son of George Lyall Chiene, a Fellow of the Royal College of Surgeons of Edinburgh (FRCSE). In 1931 he became a Writer to the Signet (WS), having served his apprenticeship under Carlyle Gifford at Baillie Gifford & Co. In 1933, he joined the firm Cowan and Dalmahoy and worked there until 1937 when he rejoined Baillie Gifford. In 1939 he married the daughter of Charles Mackinlay, an Edinburgh whisky merchant. During the Second World War he served with the Royal Artillery in France, North Africa and Italy. He reached the rank of major and was awarded the DSO.[2]

George Chiene was highly regarded in Edinburgh and in the investment trust movement. He became director of the Commercial Bank of Scotland, which in 1959 merged with the National Commercial Bank of Scotland to become the National Commercial Bank of Scotland Ltd. In 1969, The Royal Bank of Scotland Ltd was formed by the merger of The Royal Bank of Scotland and the National Commercial Bank of Scotland Ltd. Chiene also became deputy chairman of the insurance company, Scottish Life. Chiene's nephew, John Chiene Junior, later became the force behind Wood Mackenzie, a stockbroker with offices in Edinburgh that Baillie Gifford & Co dealt with.

George Chiene, who had become a partner in Baillie Gifford & Co in the late 1930s, kept out of the quarrels that were going on in the company in the late 1940s and felt that his job was to get on and manage the clients' money. However, Chiene was eventually drawn into conflict with Gifford. The proximate cause was Charles Gifford, Carlyle Gifford's son.

---

[2] Register of Society of WS, 1983.

Charles Gifford

Charles Gifford was born in October 1909 (and died in 1994). His younger brother, J. Patrick C. Gifford, was born in 1913. Patrick died in a tragic shooting accident in the summer of 1926 at Pogbie House, Humbie, the family's country home. Charles was educated at Cambridge University where he studied economics. During the war he served as the Economic Secretary at the UK Embassy in Russia.[3]

Never having been close to his father and preferring his independence, after the war Charles decided to remain in London and not join Carlyle in Baillie Gifford & Co in Edinburgh. Carlyle allowed Charles to take care of some of Baillie Gifford's business in London. [It is not clear, however, precisely what Charles' responsibilities were. From 1931 Baillie Gifford had managed the 'ecclesiasticals' in London – i.e. the Monks, Friars and Abbots investment trusts – but these trusts were managed from Edinburgh with only board meetings held in London.] The problem, however, was that while Carlyle gave Charles a significant degree of freedom, he kept George Chiene's activities under close surveillance.

Chiene resented this and eventually confronted Carlyle Gifford. Luckily for Chiene, Gifford backed down and came to the conclusion that he had to give George Chiene a reasonable degree of control and independence in Baillie Gifford & Co. Carlyle Gifford also told Charles that he had to leave Baillie Gifford. The lesson that came to be learned by the senior partners in Baillie Gifford from this incident was that although Carlyle Gifford was undoubtedly domineering – and, indeed, could be a bully – he nevertheless could be made to see reason if confronted. It may even have been the case that he gave more respect to those whom he felt were strong enough to stand up to him. In the words of Gavin Gemmell, who became senior partner in April 1989, "...the short answer was that those who could call Gifford's bluff and speak back to him found him fine to deal with but others could not cope with the pressure of constant questioning".[4]

---

[3]   At one stage while in the US, Carlyle Gifford contemplated the possibility of asking Charles to join him in carrying out his duties. Gifford (1969), p.20.
[4]   Memo by Gavin Gemmell.

1951-1969

Baillie Gifford's core business

Having negotiated a secure position for himself in charge of day-to-day decisions at Baillie Gifford & Co, George Chiene stamped his preferences firmly on the firm's activities. While Carlyle Gifford remained actively involved in the firm – incredibly, only relinquishing his chairmanship of the firm's investment trusts in 1960 by which time he was 79 years old – it was George Chiene who largely determined the firm's priorities and direction.

George Chiene and Carlyle Gifford shared a well-developed sense of caution. Based on his analyses of the British and US economies, Gifford anticipated the imminent arrival of a significant post-war recession. Chiene felt strongly that the firm should remain small and tightly focused on its core business of managing investment trusts. He believed that in this way the interests of all would be best served; clients would benefit from the focused attention of those who managed their investments while Baillie Gifford's partners were content to continue managing these assets rather than being distracted by the search for new business opportunities. This conservative and cautious approach was consistent with a steady improvement in Baillie Gifford's performance. By 1957 the firm had become the largest of the Scottish investment trust managers.[5]

Ernest Dawson and Charles White

However, it would be wrong to imagine that Chiene's views went unchallenged within the firm. Perhaps the most significant source of opposition to Chiene's anti-growth beliefs came from Ernest Dawson, the firm's *de facto* second-in-command. Dawson was born in Dundee and trained as a lawyer. Although he joined Baillie Gifford before the war, it was only after it that he became a partner. Dawson did not get on particularly well with Chiene, finding him somewhat rigid and over-bearing. Having responsibility for the firm's non-investment trust business, Dawson favoured expansion into new areas of business such as pension

---

[5]   Slaven and Checkland (1990), p.406.

funds. This was a field in which Baillie Gifford already had some experience. As early as 1948 the firm had finalised its first pension fund mandate to manage the Cadbury pension fund. In 1951 this was followed by a second mandate for the management of the pension fund of the Times Newspapers. But Chiene stymied Dawson's ambitions for growth, fearing that it would result in a loss of focus and that clients' interests would thereby be sacrificed.

However, Dawson was supported by his colleague, Charles White, who also worked on Baillie Gifford's non-investment trust businesses. J.G. Charles White was the son of an Aberdonian schoolmaster. He attended Aberdeen University, receiving a first class honours in Classics. During the war he was asked to study Japanese at London University. After an intensive one-year course, he was sent to Burma where he became involved in the interrogation of Japanese prisoners. After the war he went to Cambridge University where he did the classical tripos, obtaining another first.

Charles White joined Baillie Gifford in September 1949. In 1953 he was invited to become a partner in the firm. Charles White has left one of the few written recollections of Carlyle Gifford as a superior and colleague and his memories, tinged with emotion, provide a valuable insight not only into Gifford the man but also into the social relationships that existed at the time in Baillie Gifford & Co.[6] Furthermore, as will later be seen, his comments also provide an important understanding of one of the key components of the 'Baillie Gifford Culture'.

It is, therefore, worth reliving with Charles White the experience of joining Baillie Gifford & Co as a young investment management trainee. During the Easter of 1949 White went to Edinburgh for an interview with Baillie Gifford that had been arranged through the Cambridge University Appointments Board. He was interviewed by George Chiene, Ernest Dawson and Ian Milne, although on this occasion he did not meet Carlyle Gifford. That pleasure was to be reserved for September, several days after the new recruit first joined Baillie Gifford & Co. Charles White recalled:

---

[6]   J.G. Charles White. 'A Personal and Anecdotal Memoir of T.J. Carlyle Gifford'. 12 February 1979.

"A few days after my arrival at Glenfinlas Street, I was summoned to what (in irreverent early years) I called the Presence. I was courteously received with the words 'Pray sit down, Mr White'. (Only later did I learn that this civility could be an ominous beginning to a conversation.) Carlyle then studied some papers on his desk and suddenly said, 'Well, did you get a First?', to which I replied 'Yes'. 'Just as well', he said. I have often wondered what would have happened if I had had to say 'No'. (The explanation of this abrupt enquiry I learned only later, when I had become a Partner in the Firm, and had gained access to the staff recruitment files. At the time of my interview in the Easter Vacation I had of course still to sit Part II of the Classical Tripos, but the Appointments Board, with a fine display of confidence not shared by myself, had said that I was virtually certain to get a First.)".

Clearly, Carlyle Gifford had already become firm in his conviction that a first in classics from one of the country's distinguished universities provided an ample background for work in the rather technical area of investment analysis. As Charles White observed, "Only later did I learn that Carlyle, having seen the applications for the vacancy, had said, 'Here's a fellow who has read Classics – let's see him, and, if he's any good, take him on'".

However, his distinguished academic background provided White with little protection from Carlyle Gifford's critical scrutiny:

"After this initial encounter, I did not, as a lowly member of the staff, see Carlyle regularly for some time. As time passed, however, and I began to think with youthful presumption that I had mastered at least some of the technique of investment management, I met him from time to time when I had put up some suggestion which found favour with some of the Partners and ultimately found its way to him. I remember clearly an occasion when I had suggested that we should invest in some textile companies. This idea was accepted by some of the

Partners but was apparently ridiculed by Carlyle when he heard of it. He had asked who had initiated this preposterous idea and I was summoned to a Partners' Meeting to explain myself.

"During the confrontation I defended my suggestion and did my best to rebut adverse criticism. At length Carlyle turned to his Partners and said, 'This is a dangerous fellow; he defends himself when attacked'. Nevertheless, my idea was turned down".

Having had the misfortune to catch Gifford's attention, Charles White now had to put up with his ire:

"Not long after this episode, I was going out at lunch-time and met Carlyle emerging from his room, complete with bowler hat and umbrella. He asked me what I had done that morning. Normally this kind of question causes the mind to go completely blank, but on this occasion I was able to say that I had authorised a participation in the underwriting of an ICI [the largest British chemicals company] rights issue. To my surprise, this revelation provoked instant fury, and the umbrella whistled round my bottom in equally instant punishment. I discreetly moved down the stairs, but the punitive umbrella pursued me remorselessly. Some days later it was announced that the ICI issue had been a success, and that the underwriters had been fully relieved; but the subject was never mentioned again".

However, even this vindication did not provide the poor Charles White with respite:

"Carlyle then adopted the habit of coming to my room almost every day, just before lunch-time, to ask what I had been doing, no doubt motivated by the affair of the ICI underwriting. Normally this interrogation passed off uneventfully, but one morning I replied that I had sold 20,000 shares in AEI. This caused an immediate explosion. Never had such an imbecilic action been perpetrated in Glenfinlas Street. At one point in his tirade Carlyle picked up an old-fashioned cylindrical ruler and crashed it down on my desk to emphasise his point. By this time I had also become very angry and when Carlyle laid the ruler down, I picked it up and in turn banged it on the desk in emphasis of an argument. To this piece of unseemly obstreperousness the reply was, 'If that's how you are going to behave, you had better consider your future with the Firm very carefully'.

"With this final volley, Carlyle departed for lunch, and I did the same. I cannot recall any more wretched meal. Almost as soon as I had returned to the office, I received a dread summons to the Presence. I was invited to sit down, which I regarded as a sinister prelude. To my vast astonishment, Carlyle said, 'On reflection, I think I went too far in our conversation before lunch, and I should be greatly obliged if you would forget the whole affair'. I replied that perhaps we had both gone too far, and that I would dismiss the matter from my mind. Carlyle then went on, 'You have learned a useful lesson early, that if I am stood up to – really stood up to – I tend to crumble'. This revelation robbed me of the power of discretion, and I replied, with unintended cheek, 'Thank you, I'll remember that'. 'Devil take you', he shouted, 'get out'.

"I narrate this episode at some length because it marked a watershed in our relations. Never again did we have high words beyond the limits of civilised argument".

The contradictions of the authoritarian personality. Gifford was keen to appoint Charles White largely as a result of the latter's academic prowess, evidenced by his double first in classics. Yet, when White exercised his talents in an independent way, Gifford, out of control, was resentful. However, when authority was met by authority, Gifford tended to back down. The same had happened with George Chiene. But this was Gifford's (and therefore Baillie Gifford & Co's) saving grace since by backing down he was, ironically, able to create a space in his firm for those who were equally strong-willed. Gifford's weakness turned out also to be one of his strengths. In this way, the George Chienes and Charles Whites remained – and, indeed, triumphed with both men later becoming senior partners – even though others, such as William Watson and Ian Milne, fell by the wayside.[7]

However, it would be wrong to infer from Charles White's sometimes painful memories that Carlyle Gifford was solely a domineering bully, although at times he could certainly be. A rather different gloss is put on the Gifford-White relationship by Douglas McDougall who joined Baillie Gifford in 1965, the year he graduated from Oxford, becoming senior partner with Gavin Gemmell in April 1989. McDougall recalls that, "Carlyle enjoyed the academic atmosphere in the firm. His favourite was Charles White who got a double first in classics. He was Gifford's favourite because of his academic prowess". In the mid-1960s, McDougall remembers, "Carlyle would chair the meetings. I rather liked him. He loved repartee and a good argument. You could tease him".[8]

Douglas McDougall's recollections make it easier to understand Charles White's otherwise puzzling summing up of his feelings for Carlyle Gifford, despite the vicissitudes of the relationship:

> "The anecdotes related above do not, of course, give anything like a rounded sketch of Carlyle Gifford, and could even give a grossly misleading impression that his main attributes were ill-temper and unreason. Such an impression would be utterly grotesque. He had great gifts, and I owe him a great deal. I liked and admired him. Life in his firm was exciting and sometimes alarming, but it was never dull. We shall not see his like again".

---

[7] Unfortunately, Carlyle Gifford's son, Charles, also fell by the wayside, at least as far as Baillie Gifford & Co was concerned, although the father-son relationship must have added further layers of complexity. Although never close, Carlyle and Charles maintained contact and Carlyle frequently dined with Charles and his family in London before taking the night train back to Edinburgh, usually refusing the invitation to stay for the night. (Interview with Patrick Gifford, Charles' son.)

[8] Interview with Douglas McDougall.

This makes all the more poignant Charles White's memories of Carlyle's 90th birthday, four years before his death:[9]

"As time passed, Carlyle gradually disengaged himself from the affairs of the Firm. As did many other people, I visited him from time to time in his retirement. As he became gradually enfeebled, I found it (and I say this at the risk of being sentimental) a moving experience to visit him when bed-ridden and find my hands clasped in his while he recalled some of our earlier exchanges of views.

"The last flash of the Carlyle which I knew in previous days occurred (I think) on his ninetieth birthday, when I was invited to attend the celebration. For this occasion he was in a chair. I approached to shake his hand and offer the appropriate felicitations. Unfortunately, as I stepped forward, I trod on his toe, which I had not observed as it was concealed by an enveloping dressing-gown. This piece of ineptitude was met with the remark, 'Charles, you'll be the death of me yet'. To this was added, for the benefit of other guests, 'Here's a fellow who assaults me on my ninetieth birthday'".

Douglas McDougall's recollections of George Chiene form something of a contrast to his memories of Carlyle Gifford: "Chiene was tough. He had a temper and was short of a sense of humour. Unlike Carlyle, you could not tease him. He was humourless, rigid and dominant, but intelligent". Despite, or perhaps because of this, George Chiene was respected by Carlyle Gifford. Charles White observes that, "Carlyle had (very properly) a high regard for George", although he goes on to note that "...the high esteem in which Carlyle held him did not invariably protect him from expressions of displeasure". The following story illustrates the point:

"One especially cold day, George lit the coal fire in Carlyle's room, knowing that Carlyle was expected later

---

[9] Carlyle Gifford died on 24 January 1975 at the age of 94, ten days after his birthday.

in the morning. When Carlyle eventually appeared, and found that his fire had been lit, (a task he usually performed himself), he was furious. George was castigated for having taken such an unwarrantable liberty, and strict instructions were circulated in the office that nobody – absolutely nobody – was to put a match to Carlyle's fire except Carlyle himself. (None of Carlyle's colleagues ever understood why the lighting of his fire was a matter of such grave enormity.)".

Baillie Gifford as a professional services firm

Ernest Dawson, who it appears did not get on particularly well with George Chiene, felt strongly that Baillie Gifford should begin pursuing more seriously new markets outside its traditional business of investment trust management such as the management of pension funds. In this he received the support of his ally and friend, Charles White. However, Chiene was adamant that this was not a wise course for the firm for the reasons mentioned earlier. And he was not to be moved on this issue. In essence Chiene seems to have seen Baillie Gifford not so much as a business the purpose of which was to grow as fast as possible through the management of the investments of others, but rather as a professional services company, like a law firm, whose aim was to do a professional and reasonably lucrative job serving the interests of its clients.

As Gavin Gemmell – who became senior partner with Douglas McDougall in April 1989, having joined the firm in 1964 – put it, "Management of clients' portfolios was the whole business in George Chiene's view.... One or two new clients...were taken on but others were turned down and no active selling took place.... Fees were either fixed or business value related and there was a tendency to delay increasing investment trust fees if the business was profitable due to new clients. In effect the business was being run as a collection of salaries or a co-operative for the investment trusts and bottom line profits depended quite heavily on non-executive directors fees of Gifford and Chiene".[10] However, as already noted, while this approach did not result in a rapidly

---

[10] Memo by Gavin Gemmell.

growing firm, Baillie Gifford still became by 1957 Scotland's largest investment trust manager.

Carlyle Gifford relinquishes control

In 1960, aged 79, Carlyle Gifford relinquished chairmanship of the six Scottish investment trusts managed by Baillie Gifford. At this point he remained "…the sole governing partner and owned all the equity and stock [in Baillie Gifford and Co]". According to Gavin Gemmell, "…it is generally believed that this was not because he did not want to share the profits and his colleagues received good incomes, but he wished to have complete control. When, in his 80s he decided to relinquish control, he then made over the buildings which were owned by the firm to his colleagues at cost price which seemed to confirm that it was not a question of greed. Nevertheless, it does give a picture of somebody who could be quite overbearing and it was fortunate for the firm that George Chiene had the measure of him".[11]

On 4 May 1960, some time after the death of his first wife Maud, Carlyle Gifford married Sophia Mary Wharton Millar, the daughter of an advocate, John Hepburn Millar, who was Professor of Constitutional Law at the University of Edinburgh from 1909-1925. Sophia particularly enjoyed tennis and golf (sports that Gifford regularly enjoyed whilst in the US, as recorded in his letters). In 1938 she won the Ladies Championship in golf in Sweden. Far younger than Gifford, Sophia died on 16 August 1991.[12]

Baillie Gifford merges its investment trusts

From 1968, a time of booming UK equity prices,[13] Baillie Gifford decided to merge the investment trusts it managed forming three larger entities. This is shown in Exhibit 4.1.

---

[11] ibid.

[12] University of Edinburgh Bulletin, http://www.cpa.ed.ac.uk/bulletinarchive/1991-1992/01/obituaries.html

[13] For example, in this year Standard Life decided to invest 60% of all the new money it received in equities. Moss (2000), p.265.

Exhibit 4.1. Baillie Gifford's three merged investment trusts

Date	Name	Former Investment Trusts
1968	Monks Investment Trust	• Abbots Investment Trust • Friars Investment Trust • Monks Investment Trust
1969	Scottish Mortgage Investment Trust	• Scottish Mortgage and Trust • Second Scottish Mortgage and Trust • Scottish Capital Investment
1969	Edinburgh and Dundee Investment Co	• Edinburgh, Dundee and Aberdeen Investment • Second Edinburgh and Dundee Investment • Scottish Central Investment Trust

However, although the reorganisation generated managerial economies, "George Chiene was very keen that the benefit of less meetings went to management of investment trusts, not business expansion of Baillie Gifford".[14]

---

[14] Memo by Gavin Gammell.

Review of the period

In reviewing this period, with the benefit of hindsight, two points stand out. The first is the formation of key features of what will be referred to here as the 'Baillie Gifford Culture'. The second is the ideological limits on growth imposed on the firm by George Chiene. The relationship between these two points will be considered later.

The 'Baillie Gifford Culture'

Perhaps the most important feature of the 'Baillie Gifford Culture' is the firm's partnership mode of governance. Although by no means uncommon in this period, at the present time in the financial world – including both the US and UK – partnerships have become something of an anachronism. The reasons for this important phenomenon will not be explored further here. Comment will be confined to several observations on the viability of the partnership form of governance in the case of Baillie Gifford during the period of its history currently under review, namely from 1951 to 1969.

Possibly the most significant characteristic of the partnership mode of governance is that it holds out the possibility for a skilled employee to become a secure and relatively well-remunerated member of a thriving community. Of course, not all those employed by Baillie Gifford achieved partnership status, although amongst the individuals discussed in this section the common pattern was to be invited to become a partner within four or five years of joining the firm. The prospect of security and pay seems to have been sufficient to prevent these individuals from exiting the firm, despite the pressures that they must have been put under by the domineering personalities of Carlyle Gifford and George Chiene. However, although at this time many other professional firms may have exhibited similar social relationships, the departure of people like William Watson and Ian Milne in the late 1940s shows that not everyone felt that the price of membership of Baillie Gifford & Co was worth paying at this point in time.

Nevertheless, for those willing to pay the price during this period, the rewards seem to have provided more than sufficient compensation. As in most families, the 'ups' more than outweighed the 'downs'. Both Ernest Dawson and Charles White went on to become senior partners. The former led Baillie Gifford from April 1972, when he replaced George Chiene, until April 1975 when he himself was replaced by Charles White who led the firm until April 1983, giving way to Angus Millar. And the retention rate amongst the ordinary partners, less visible than the senior partners and with less controlling power, remained high.

Significantly, at this stage partnership did not mean common ownership. As already noted, until the 1960s Carlyle Gifford was the sole owner of Baillie Gifford & Co, owning the firm's equity, stock and building, and was formally the sole governing partner, even though, as we have seen, significant *de facto* power was devolved to George Chiene. In short, common ownership was not one of the rewards that held the partnership together during this period.

The second characteristic of the 'Baillie Gifford Culture' was the intellectual calibre of many of the firm's recruits. For all his shortcomings, Carlyle Gifford was committed to recruiting bright, creative people, even though he had as a consequence no option but to put up with the results of their intelligence. This characteristic of the firm was to become one of its distinguishing features, as will be seen, in later periods.

The ideological limits on growth

However, the quality of Baillie Gifford's staff was not sufficient under George Chiene's leadership to generate an endogenous drive for growth. Chiene kept a tight lid on this impetus. However, as will become apparent later, this ideological approach would not survive the period of Chiene's leadership.

1970-1976

The beginnings of change

According to Gavin Gemmell, who joined Baillie Gifford in 1964 and became senior partner in April 1989, "The beginnings of modern Baillie Gifford began about 1972".[15] Until this time, as Gemmell pointed out later, "...we didn't perceive ourselves as managing a business. We considered ourselves more like a firm of

---

[15] Memo by Gavin Gemmell.

solicitors managing our clients' affairs without much focus on running those of our own".[16]

Why did a significant change begin occurring from about 1972? What were the forces behind this change? One factor was that George Chiene, who as we have seen resolutely opposed significant growth in the firm including growth in new areas of business, retired in April 1972 and was replaced by Ernest Dawson. Dawson had been responsible for Baillie Gifford's non-investment trust business and favoured growth in this and other areas of new business. However, significantly, the change in Baillie Gifford was not simply the result of new leadership.

According to Gemmell,[17] there were several fundamental internal transformations taking place in Baillie Gifford, intrinsically linked to the gradually changing nature of the firm and the industry of which it was a part, that were the main drivers of change. These transformations were expressed in the need for additional resources. In Gemmell's words, "There was a feeling at the time that we needed more resources".

These were needed for several purposes. To begin with, Ernest Dawson felt it was necessary to expand the number of new trainees and therefore the overall number of staff. There were two related reasons for more staff. First, it was felt that it was important to increase the amount of in-house research done in the firm. As Gemmell noted, "As a company we took research seriously". As Baillie Gifford's funds under management expanded so it became necessary to increase the number of researchers. Secondly, "We were covering more of the world – Japan and Europe in addition to the UK and US", and this added to the need for more researchers. [For example, Baillie Gifford began investing in Japan in 1963 although it was only in 1981, with the establishment of the Baillie Gifford Japan Trust, that a Japanese country team was established.]

A further reason for more resources came from the advent of new technology. With the development of computer technology expensive databases became not only available but also essential to assist with research and evaluation of individual companies and

---

[16] Quoted in *Financial Times*, 6 April 1988.
[17] Interview with Gavin Gemmell.

portfolios. Examples were those provided by Datastream and Reuters.

In order to pay for increased staff, information technology and information the investment trusts were asked to pay substantially increased fees. However, although this slowly began to change the nature of the firm, turning it more into an investment management business rather than a fee-charging professional services company, it did not yet produce a strong impetus to grow the firm's range of customers and to enter decisively into new market segments such as pension funds. Gavin Gemmell's observations on the overall attitude in Baillie Gifford when he joined the firm remained still largely accurate, even though the draughts of change were now beginning to stir: "The atmosphere when I joined in the 1960s was definitely non-entrepreneurial and rather frustrating for anyone keen to build a business".[18]

Early pension fund mandates

One example of slowly stirring change was the gradually increasing importance of pension fund mandates. As noted earlier, Baillie Gifford's first pension fund mandate was that of the confectionery company, Cadbury, concluded in 1948. This was followed in 1951 with the Times Newspapers (apparently a Baillie Gifford staff member had a friend in the City who recommended the firm to Times, hardly an example of intentional marketing). In the early 1950s Charles White visited Glaxo, the British pharmaceuticals company. The reason for the visit was that Baillie Gifford held a significant number of Glaxo shares. However, Glaxo, on the strength of the contact with White, invited Baillie Gifford to manage some of its pension funds, although George Chiene turned this opportunity down since the proposal was not consistent with his view of the firm's priorities.[19]

However, by the late 1960s Baillie Gifford had acquired a number of pension and charity fund mandates. These included Birmingham and Edinburgh Universities as well as Venesta, a plywood company, and Darchem, an engineering company based

---

[18] Memo by Gavin Gemmell.
[19] Interview with Max Ward.

in Darlington which was involved in asbestos and electricity insulation products.

Although limited and still not a significant contributor to funds under management these early pension fund activities began to generate the competencies and orientation that would later facilitate a far more decisive move into the pension fund management market. In 1974 Gavin Gemmell took over the management of all 'gross funds' (i.e. tax-exempt funds that included pension funds that paid neither income nor capital gains tax, in contrast to investment trusts that had to pay capital gains tax from 1965). As he recalls, "I established links with major actuarial firms and did some cold calling but it was not consistent and [my] main task was investing more actively and attending meetings for about 10 clients".[20] Clearly, the marketing of Baillie Gifford's management services to pension funds was not yet a priority in the firm. He adds, "We paid insufficient attention to advice from John Chiene [George Chiene's nephew] that one person full-time on marketing is much better than 2/3 people part time".

Death of Carlyle Gifford

On 24 January 1975 Carlyle Gifford died aged 94. In two senses his death marked the end of an era. Not only had the second of Baillie Gifford's two founders died, the firm was, coincidentally, about to be thrust abruptly into a new era that would pose the severest challenge it had ever confronted and then lead it into a period of radical change and unprecedented prosperity.

1977-1984: THE CREATIVE CRISIS

The 1977 Takeover of the Edinburgh and Dundee Investment Company

In 1977, in a bolt out of the blue, Baillie Gifford was hit by the worst catastrophe it had ever faced. In one day the firm lost about one-quarter of its assets under management, plunging its partners into a severe crisis. In dealing urgently with the effects of this

---

[20] Memo by Gavin Gemmell.

crisis the partners had no option but to re-examine fundamentally the principles on which Baillie Gifford had been based.

At the end of 1974 the London stock market collapsed as the Labour Government, re-elected in October 1974, failed in its attempts to tackle escalating inflation. By the end of 1974 the FT Actuaries index had fallen 54%. The market had been driven down steadily by rising oil prices and rising nominal interest rates (though falling real rates) caused gilts to suffer. In July 1975 inflation reached a peak.

In the midst of these events Ernest Dawson retired as senior partner and was replaced by Charles White. The time was not good for Baillie Gifford. Not only was the firm, like other fund managers, hit by the adverse financial conditions, it did not perform well relative to its peers. According to *The Economist*: "Managers Baillie Gifford have been one of the least distinguished performers in *The Economist's* surveys over the years".[21]

It was against this background that the crisis struck. The lightning bolt took the form of the takeover of the Edinburgh and Dundee Investment Company,[22] until then managed by Baillie Gifford, by the British Rail Pension Fund. The reason for the loss of the Edinburgh and Dundee Investment Co was that, as a result of the financial difficulties of 1976, the discounts on investment trusts were very wide. The British Rail Pension Fund took advantage of these circumstances and acquired the trust. Unfortunately for Baillie Gifford, the firm had not anticipated the possibility of such action and accordingly had not built up a defence.

Needless to say, the partners and the rest of the Baillie Gifford staff were devastated on hearing the news. However, as things turned out, the devastation produced the fuel for a series of responses and reforms that would, over time, lay the foundation for

---

[21] *The Economist*, 16 August 1975.

[22] The Edinburgh and Dundee Investment Co was formed in 1969 through the merging of Edinburgh, Dundee and Aberdeen Investment Co (1914) (National Archives of Scotland, GD 376, 1914-1977), the Second Edinburgh and Dundee Investment Co (1927) (National Archives of Scotland, GD 376, 1927-1969) and the Scottish Central Investment Trust. See Exhibit 4.1 above.

the Baillie Gifford of today, a foundation conducive to steady growth in assets under management, partners, staff and profits.

How did the partners respond? The first response, not un-expectedly particularly for such an intellectual firm, was to debate the alternatives. In doing so the partners quickly arrived at a consensus. According to Richard Burns – who joined the firm in 1973, becoming a partner in 1977 and senior partner in April 1999 – the consensus was summarised in the phrase that became common currency at the time in Baillie Gifford: "Are we gentlemen or are we in business?".[23]

The pressures produced by the substantial fall in assets under management helped to answer this rhetorical question. However, while the option of being gentlemen might have seemed anachronistic, the question raised a further more complex question regarding the alternative; what needs to be done in order to be 'in business'? The answer that Baillie Gifford had until 1977 given to this question was at the stroke of a takeover agreement rendered obsolete. As Max Ward noted (having joined the firm in October 1971 and being appointed as partner in 1974), "When I joined Baillie Gifford there was the belief that firms that took on new business compromised their service standards to existing clients".[24] But what new interpretation, in the light of the events of 1977, was needed regarding what it now should mean to be 'in business'?

Response to Crisis

Contesting the pension fund market

As Richard Burns and Max Ward recalled,[25] the partners realised that their existing business, now built primarily on the management of only three investment trusts, did not provide sufficient security. Quite apart from the threat of takeover of the investment trusts, the large discount on the trusts in the context of poor stock market performance left little room for regaining lost ground by expanding the funds managed in the investment trusts remaining in the Baillie Gifford stable. In the words of Gavin

---

[23] Interview with Richard Burns.
[24] Interview with Max Ward.
[25] Interviews with Richard Burns and Max Ward.

Gemmell, "After Edinburgh and Dundee disappeared, it was recognised that we would have to go into pensions in a more serious way. It was recognised that funds under management in our remaining investment trusts could not be greatly expanded because of the large discount that existed".[26]

This necessitated that attention be shifted to new areas of business beyond the firm's hitherto core business of investment trust management. Fortunately, as noted earlier, Baillie Gifford had not entirely ignored other markets such as pension funds even if they were not accorded priority. Unfortunately, however, in the late-1970s Baillie Gifford's pension fund business was not doing particularly well.

For example, although the firm retained the management mandate for funds such as those of Edinburgh and Birmingham Universities, and although some new business had been obtained, three of its earliest mandates had been lost. The Cadbury mandate, the firm's first pension fund mandate originally obtained in 1948, was lost after indifferent performance and after Baillie Gifford was outperformed by Kleinwort (which also managed some of Cadbury's pension funds). A new finance director at Cadbury decided to end Baillie Gifford's mandate. In the case of the Times Newspapers, initially agreed in 1951, the mandate ended when the Times' pension fund was amalgamated with the Thomson Organisation Scheme.[27] The Venesta mandate was lost after the firm went into bankruptcy.[28] In the none-too-optimistic words of Max Ward, summarising the situation that existed at the time, "We were sinking further back".[29]

But adversity can give birth to its opposite if it creates the motivation and incentive to change things for the better. One of the benefits of Baillie Gifford's adversity in the wake of the loss of the Edinburgh and Dundee Investment Co was that it forced the partners to look openly and honestly in the mirror. And, in a mood of honest reflection, they had to admit that they were not entirely happy with the image they saw. Max Ward articulated one of the

---

[26] Interview with Gavin Gemmell.
[27] Memo by Gavin Gemmell.
[28] Interview with Gavin Gemmell.
[29] Interview with Max Ward.

self-criticisms: "We were complacent!".[30] Furthermore, the partners were forced to recognise that they had not paid sufficient attention to performance.

To make matters even worse, some of Baillie Gifford's major counterparts and competitors in Edinburgh were doing extremely well. To quote Max Ward again: "At that time, Ivory & Sime were going from strength to strength and Martin Currie were doing well. We were the smallest of the three in the early '80s in terms of assets under management. We were definitely the laggards".[31]

However, the crisis also had the effect of making the partners gird their loins: "There was a real sense that we had nothing to lose. The whole mood of the organisation was receptive to radical solution".[32] As Richard Burns starkly put it, "Baillie Gifford could have gone under".[33] And if anything could concentrate the mind and facilitate an abrupt break with the past, this prospect could. Within this context, options that had previously been overlooked or ignored – whether through complacency, inertia or because they ran counter to the strong convictions of George Chiene – were raised, re-examined and investigated.

In my interviews with key Baillie Gifford partners I was keen to probe deeper into the process of crisis in the firm at this watershed time. Crises are particularly important junctures in the evolution of organisations. Because of their nature, crises can have the effect of alleviating, if not removing, the deadweight of history, opening up possibilities that hitherto were perceived to be impossible. But, notoriously, crises often also result in the crumbling of leadership, power structures and alliances and therefore can provoke times of intense conflict. The reason, simply, is that crises often produce new threats but all in the organisation are not equally threatened and different options distribute threat and opportunity differently amongst an organisation's members. I was therefore interested to find out whether, in the aftermath of the Edinburgh and Dundee Investment Co takeover, there were major conflicts and debates and, if so, what their substance was.

---

[30] ibid.
[31] ibid.
[32] ibid.
[33] Interview with Richard Burns.

Through my questions, however, I discovered, remarkably, that there was minimal conflict though a good amount of debate took place about the options and their consequences. Max Ward spoke for all when he said that, "We realised that we did not have secure business and that we must have new business. We started to worry about performance and promoting ourselves. There was absolute unanimity about the new direction".[34]

But this absence of conflict itself needs to be explained. Several factors, taken together, provide the explanation. The first is that after the takeover it was immediately made clear, as Gavin Gemmell recalled, that "...there would be no forced redundancies, although a few people decided to leave".[35] Secondly, as far as the partners were concerned, the institution of partnership had the effect, not only of putting everyone in the same boat, but producing the motivation and incentive to stay in the boat and pull together in order to find a way out of the rough waters. In short, in the words of Albert O. Hirschmann,[36] partnership encouraged the exercising of voice and loyalty rather than exit. With everyone firmly seated in the same boat it was possible to develop a consensus regarding how to navigate a way out.

And the outlines of the navigation strategy soon became clear. In particular, it was agreed that the pension fund market must immediately become a priority. But this raised further issues that, in turn, imposed further requirements. As Richard Burns put it, "In order to develop pension fund management we needed good performance in UK equities [because a significant proportion of the assets of pension funds were invested in UK equities]. This required people working full-time on UK equities. Max Ward, who was most bullish about UK equities, was put in charge".[37]

---

[34] Interview with Max Ward. When pushed further over the last sentence, Ward added, "I was unaware of major internal conflict over the [1977] crisis".

[35] Interview with Gavin Gemmell.

[36] Hirschmann, A.O. 1970. *Exit, Voice and Loyalty: Responses to decline in firms, organizations and states.*

[37] Interview with Richard Burns.

Max Ward[38]

Max Ward studied mathematics at St Catharine's College, Cambridge. He joined Baillie Gifford in October 1971 immediately after graduating. His father was a stockbroker working with Vickers da Costa, one of the leading London stockbrokers. The family assumption was that Max would work in financial services in London. However, in searching through job opportunities in the Cambridge University jobs office Max happened upon a roneo copy advertising an employment opportunity at Baillie Gifford in Edinburgh. Max loved Scotland. His mother was Scottish and his grandfather had lived in Shetland. However, his father was Irish and thought of himself as Irish. Nevertheless, his father strongly supported the idea of Max applying for the Baillie Gifford job. Baillie Gifford was one of Max's father's clients at Vickers da Costa and he thought that the firm was outstanding, with extremely talented people. Furthermore, he thought that the quality of life was superior in Edinburgh to that of London.

Although he got along very well with colleagues such as Angus Millar and Douglas MacDougall, "My first few years at Baillie Gifford were difficult. It was only in about my third year that people began to take my views seriously and listen to me". However, in 1974 Max was offered a partnership, to take effect from 1975: "In those days people expected partnerships to last for life".

Charged with re-vitalising Baillie Gifford's UK equities performance, Max Ward, perhaps drawing on his mathematics background, brought increased rigour to the task. According to Gavin Gemmell, "Max took the analysis of companies to the next level".[39] In an interview with the author, Ward summarised his approach: "My approach was to build portfolios based on a rigorous analysis of companies without regard to the composition of the index. We had to look to our own judgment". But he also acknowledged the difficulties that this approach implied: "This involved huge risk if you got it wrong". However, here too Baillie

---

[38] This section is based largely on an interview with Max Ward.
[39] Interview with Gavin Gemmell.

Gifford's 1977 crisis proved to be beneficial: "The fact that we were already losing our business paradoxically made it easier".

Going out into the world

If one of the necessary conditions for contesting the pension fund market was to improve the organisation and performance of Baillie Gifford's UK equities team, another requirement was to make the firm and its competencies more visible in the market. Indeed, the crisis also served to bring out into the open how inward looking and relatively isolated Baillie Gifford had become. This was one of the hidden costs of the George Chiene regime. Although the firm's core business focused on investment trusts may have kept the partners and investment managers and analysts busy and comfortably remunerated, and although clients' interests were being looked after, this also produced a degree of complacence and inwardness. Now, in the aftermath of the crisis, the firm had no option but to go out and sell itself. In turn, this new engagement with the market would produce a range of unanticipated, though beneficial, dynamic effects.

According to Richard Burns,[40] this "...was a crucial turning point for Baillie Gifford. It was the first time we sold something successfully. We met many people in the City [of London]. It did wonders for staff morale, that had been battered by the takeover of Edinburgh and Dundee". Gavin Gemmell expressed a similar view: "Although the bid [by the British Rail Pension Fund for Edinburgh and Dundee] was successful, the high profile defence was stimulating. The investment community (in London particularly) became aware of the energetic and high calibre personnel in [Baillie Gifford] and some useful contacts were made. Morale was low amongst staff but partners realised that the opportunities were there if we could grasp them".[41]

The positive knock-on effects produced by the crisis also affected the substance of Baillie Gifford's approach to investment strategy in general and also to its core business in investment trusts. As Gemmell noted, "[The crisis] was the catalyst to a more aggressive risk taking investment strategy. It was clear that for

---

[40]   Interview with Richard Burns.
[41]   Memo by Gavin Gemmell.

investment trusts, a middle of the road strategy was not wanted by institutional shareholders".[42]

Given the opportunity to display the competencies that had hitherto been largely concealed, Baillie Gifford was able to repair some of the damage that the takeover of the Edinburgh and Dundee Investment Co had inflicted. As a result of the initial selling campaign, Richard Burns recalled, £10 million was added to the £340 million that Baillie Gifford already managed.[43] The result was a new feeling of self-confidence. As Gavin Gemmell put it, "When we tried to sell ourselves in London we saw that we really did have talent".[44]

Globalisation - Japan

Harking back to the days when Scottish investment trusts had emerged and grown on the back of investment opportunities overseas – for example, railways in the US in the late 19th century, or, in Baillie Gifford's own case, rubber in Malaya – the firm had quietly accumulated investment expertise in the Japanese market. Indeed, Baillie Gifford was one of the early UK investment managers to develop the competencies[45] to invest in Japan.[46]

According to Max Ward, it was Ernest Dawson who first motivated the move into Japanese investments. Here he must have been assisted by Charles White, whom as we have seen became fluent in Japanese during the war as a result of his involvement with the security forces. [Indeed, Ernest Dawson was married to a Japanese woman for a time.] At any rate, Gavin Gemmell recalls that when he joined Baillie Gifford in 1964 the company held

---

[42] ibid.

[43] Interview with Richard Burns.

[44] Interview with Gavin Gemmell.

[45] These competencies, it is worth noting, have as much to do with the development of information-facilitating institutional networks as they do the development of in-house competencies embodied in experts on Japanese investments. As with UK investments in the US in the latter part of the 19th century, the former as much as the latter explain the ability of investment managers, sitting in the UK where they are far away from their 'target' country, to earn adequate rates of return from their investments in far-off places.

[46] Vickers da Costa, the London stock-broking firm for which Max Ward's father worked, was another early UK entrant into the Japanese market as was Jardine Fleming.

shares in four Japanese companies; Hitachi (electronics), Takeda (pharmaceuticals), Teijin (which began as a rayon producer) and one other.[47]

By 1981 Baillie Gifford's competencies on Japan allowed the firm to establish the Baillie Gifford Japan Trust. At the same time a formal Japan team was established, consolidating the firm's expertise in this area. Although Baillie Gifford's Japanese investments were motivated mainly by the hope for attractive rates of return from this rapidly-growing 'emerging' country, the firm, as will be seen, was also to benefit from unanticipated spin-off effects from its expertise on Japan. More specifically, this expertise would turn out to provide Baillie Gifford with a differentiating distinctive competence as it began contesting the US market for managed funds.

Globalisation - US

Contesting the UK pension funds markets was at this time, as Gavin Gemmell recalls, a difficult business. To begin with, there were many larger, stronger competitors. Furthermore, as already noted, Baillie Gifford's track record in UK equities was at this stage not particularly strong. However, emboldened by their new-found confidence, the firm's leaders decided to make a play for the US market.

Was the move into the US foresightful or foolish? Gemmell remembers that according to the conventional wisdom that then ruled, "For a fund manager to successfully enter the US market one needed 3 US clients, 3 years and at least $300 million under management".[48] Unfortunately, Baillie Gifford only possessed the third of these requirements. However, this did not prevent the firm from trying its luck in the US market. Some encouragement was derived from "…our hope that because US pension funds tended to use more outside managers of their funds than in the UK, they would be more open to smaller niche managers [like Baillie Gifford]".[49]

---

[47] Interview with Gavin Gemmell.
[48] Interview with Gavin Gemmell.
[49] ibid.

In 1983 Angus Millar, Gavin Gemmell and Robin Menzies went to the US: "We saw no point in visiting large players like Citibank, J.P. Morgan, etc. So we visited regional banks in places like Chicago, San Francisco and Dallas".[50] Fortunately, one of these regional banks responded positively. The Republic Bank in Dallas recognised that their clients wanted international investments. The bank had been trying unsuccessfully to team up with Fidelity. The outcome, in June 1983, was that the Republic Bank and Baillie Gifford agreed that the bank would set up a pooled fund consisting of $10 million which the latter would manage. This was Baillie Gifford's first US client.

Significantly, this fund performed well. One of the main reasons was the significant gains registered by the Japanese stock exchange. However, shortly thereafter the Republic Bank was struck by oil-related problems that hit Texas and the consequent collapse in real estate prices. As a result, the bank went bankrupt. Baillie Gifford's first customer turned out also to be its first false start in the US. [The Republic Bank then became part of the North Carolina National Bank which itself later became part of the Bank of America.] Nevertheless, the Republic Bank International Fund continued in existence.

In 1985, Baillie Gifford succeeded in getting its second US client, the Rockwell Corporation, a defence contractor. After the necessary negotiations, Susan Leathers in Rockwell's headquarters made the decision to give Baillie Gifford a pension fund of $100 million to manage. According to Gavin Gemmell, the Rockwell mandate was a "stroke of luck".[51] Unfortunately, however, this relationship was not to last very long. After the 1987 stock market crash, Rockwell decided to sell all the equities held in the pension fund and this ended its relationship with Baillie Gifford. For Richard Burns, Rockwell ended up being Baillie Gifford's "second false start" in the US.[52]

It was only after Ross Lidstone took over US marketing on a full-time basis that Baillie Gifford made its effective entry into the US market. Unlike other UK investment managers that opened up

---

[50] ibid.
[51] Memo by Gavin Gemmell.
[52] Interview with Richard Burns.

and staffed expensive offices based in the US, Baillie Gifford's tactics were to have its marketers based in Edinburgh with relatively modest budgets. The advantage of this approach was that close coordination was maintained with the other Baillie Gifford staff in Edinburgh whose competencies provided the raw material that the marketers would have to turn into a source of competitive advantage in the US. [All of Baillie Gifford's investment staff have always been based in a single location in Edinburgh, which the firm sees as one of its distinctive advantages, facilitating as it does close coordination and communication.] As Ross Lidstone was later to explain, "Our clients are spread globally and our preferred route into new markets has always been through joint ventures with established local players, rather than opening our own offices".[53]

Organisational Consequences

Baillie Gifford's response to the 1977 crisis, therefore, took the firm decisively into the pension fund market, both in the UK as well as in the US. In the latter market, its growing strength in Japanese equities was an important source of competitive advantage. However, these moves were also to have significant consequences for the firm's internal organisational structure.

Country- and region-based teams

In the 1960s, stock picking was organised in sectors such as capital goods, consumer goods, financials, etc. According to Richard Burns, "If a capital goods sector company was being considered then a person from the capital goods sector team would provide an input in deciding how many of that company's shares should be held in the different portfolios in Baillie Gifford".[54]

However, with the expansion of Baillie Gifford's business beyond investment trusts the disadvantages of this form of organisation soon became apparent. One significant problem, as Gavin Gemmell noted in an interview with the author, was that in each sector attention tended to focus on US firms. The reason was

---

[53] *Financial News*, 12 February 2001.
[54] Interview with Richard Burns.

not only that these firms were often the most dynamic and rapidly growing in the sector viewed from a global perspective. A further reason was that research on American firms, largely coming out of the US itself, tended to be more rigorous than that available for UK, European and Japanese firms.

The result was that the latter firms could be crowded out by the American firms in the competition for the attention of investors and researchers. However, although US companies constituted an important part of many of Baillie Gifford's port-folios, as we have seen UK pension funds demanded that most of their assets be held in UK equities and many pension funds – Baillie Gifford's US clients in particular – wanted to hold some Japanese equities and increasingly European equities too. As Richard Burns more succinctly explained, the move from a sector to a country-based form of organisation was done: "Because we needed good results in UK equities".[55]

Max Ward pointed to a further shortcoming of the sector-based form of organisation: "Initial attempts to create investment managers [based on sectors] were not very successful. Too many industrial sub-sectors existed resulting in a lack of decisiveness".[56] Precisely the same point was made by Gavin Gemmell.[57]

These drawbacks associated with sector-based organisation led to the gradual evolution of a new way of organising investment and research decisions, namely one based on country (and, in the case of Europe and later the Pacific Basin, regional) teams. By 1980 country teams had been established for the UK, US and Japan. However, according to Gemmell,[58] the transition from a sector- to a country-based organisation was gradual and some people continued to specialise in sectors (such as in the case of the oil sector).[59] In Gemmell's view: "So far as investment manage-

---

[55] ibid. As noted earlier, Max Ward was put in charge of the UK equities team.
[56] Interview with Max Ward.
[57] Gavin Gemmell, 'Thoughts on Planning' (1987?).
[58] Interview with Gavin Gemmell.
[59] Somewhat ironically, as will later be shown, in 2003 Baillie Gifford established a Global Team to complement the existing country teams in response to the demand from some pension funds and other clients for a global analysis of companies in particular sectors such as electronics and pharmaceuticals. (Interview with Richard Burns.)

ment is concerned the mainly geographical teams and the clearer delegation of decision making were the key changes made in 1980".[60]

The Institutional Clients Department

In the evolutionary process of corporate change a firm, in adapting to its changing environment, confronts further pressures and incentives for internal change that, in turn, impact on its fitness, its ability to survive and prosper under the selection processes that are an essential part of this environment. In responding to its 1977 crisis, as has been seen, Baillie Gifford went out and more pro-actively sold its competencies. The result was a steadily increasing list of pension fund clients, both in the UK and in the US as documented earlier.

The management of this relationship raises a conflict for investment managers in terms of the diversion of time and attention away from the management of the client's investments. In short, there is a trade-off; the more time spent reporting to the client (e.g. preparing the reporting documentation and meeting with the client) the less time there is for active management of the client's portfolio. And clearly, the greater the number of clients per investment manager, the greater the problem becomes.

It was in response to this conflict that Baillie Gifford introduced an important organisational innovation. In essence, the innovation involved the separation of the stock-picking value investment function from the functions of overall resource allocation (i.e. allocating the funds in the portfolio to different asset classes), selling, monitoring performance and reporting to clients.[61] These two different sets of functions were performed by different people. In short, the innovation involved a process of managerial and organisational specialisation. As a result of the innovation the stock-picking value investment managers were able to give greater focus and attention to their task.

However, initially, this innovation was difficult to introduce, as Max Ward recalls.[62] The reason was that clients had come to

---

[60] Gavin Gemmell, 'Thoughts on Planning', (1987?), p.3.

[61] Interviews with Gavin Gemmell and Max Ward.

[62] Interview with Max Ward.

expect that they would have ready access to the people involved in all aspects of the management of their investments. To be told that this access would be limited was for some clients a cause for concern. But, in overcoming this hurdle, Baillie Gifford was conveniently assisted by its crisis of 1977. Having lost important pension fund clients such as the Times Newspapers and Cadbury, Baillie Gifford was able to make the organisational change while minimising the disappointment of clients.[63] It remained for Baillie Gifford to sell the innovation to new clients.

Gavin Gemmell explains the process: "We used this innovation as a selling point with clients. We asked them, 'Do you want a person working only half-time on your portfolio?' We might take Max [Ward] to clients to explain how he goes about his work [of stock picking]. But we added, 'You won't see much of him'".[64] According to Max Ward, the innovation was an important source of improved performance for Baillie Gifford, although he readily acknowledges that what he calls 'Mother Fortune' also played a role.[65]

It was this organisational innovation that led to the establishment of the Institutional Clients Department. Although novel at the time, and seen by Baillie Gifford as a distinctive source of competitiveness, the practice has been widely adopted (though not universally) by the investment management community.[66]

---

[63] ibid.

[64] Interview with Gavin Gemmell.

[65] Interview with Max Ward.

[66] The introduction by Baillie Gifford of the Institutional Clients Department is in some important respects similar to that significant corporate innovation, the introduction of the so-called M-Form – or multidivisional form – of corporate organisation. As Professors Alfred Chandler, the doyen of business history, and Oliver Williamson have shown, the M-Form of organisation played a central role in freeing the attention of the CEOs of large corporations from preoccupation with the regular operations of the company's several divisions, allowing them to focus on more fundamental issues vital for the future of the company as a whole. Baillie Gifford's Institutional Clients Department played a not-dissimilar role.

Angus Millar

In April 1983 Charles White retired as senior partner and was replaced by Angus Millar. Angus George Millar was born on July 1928, the son of George William Russell Millar, a rubber planter based in Port Dickson, Malay States. He went to school at Loretto and from there won a scholarship to do a BA at Oxford University. He later completed a Bachelor of Law (LL.B) degree. He became a Writer to the Signet (WS) in 1955, having served as apprentice to Carlyle Gifford and others at Baillie Gifford. In 1959 he married Julia Mary Cathcart, the daughter of Alan Cathcart of Drumgrange, Kirkcudbrightshire.[67] Angus Millar had worked closely with Gavin Gemmell on the amalgamation of the three London 'ecclesiasticals' and the consolidations of Scottish Mortgage and Edinburgh and Dundee. Although "Angus was not well known either in Edinburgh or in the investment trust world at large…it was during Angus' period that the firm began to really take off".[68] One indicator of this was the establishment of the European Department in 1984.

The European Department

At this time equities in other European countries tended not to be taken seriously by most UK investment managers. Part of the reason was the good performance of UK equities. For example, in 1979 Standard Life, based in Edinburgh like Baillie Gifford, decided to return to equities that it had avoided since the UK stock market crash in 1974. By March 1982 the expected return on equities had improved to such an extent that Standard Life decided to stop all further free fund investment in fixed-interest securities.[69]

In 1984 Baillie Gifford established a European Department for investment in European equities in response to demand from the firm's new US clients. It was James Anderson, who joined Baillie Gifford in 1981, who proposed the establishment of this department and went on to head it. About one-third of the initial

---

[67] Register of Society of WS, 1983.
[68] Memo by Gavin Gemmell.
[69] Moss (2000), pp.289 and 305.

funds went into German financial assets (which later benefited Baillie Gifford when German equities outperformed UK equities).[70]

1985-PRESENT: FROM STRENGTH TO STRENGTH

Baillie Gifford's Business Plan in the Mid-1980s

At the end of 1986, Gavin Gemmell wrote a memorandum that referred, amongst other things, to Baillie Gifford's "...new business plan for the last few years".[71] This plan included the following six points:

"1. Set up new IT's [investment trusts] when possible
2. Build up UK pension fund business
3. Build up US pension business if possible with limited allocation of manpower
4. Develop exempt funds [unit trusts for UK tax-exempt funds] if possible and build up public authorised unit trusts
5. Keep our ears open for European pension funds
6   Speak to any potential partners in managing Japanese money".

Baillie Gifford (and the other major Scottish investment trust managers) had already made significant progress in the area of investment trusts. In 1983, for example, it was reported that while the total assets of all British investment trusts amounted to £14 billion, £5 billion of this (i.e. 36%) was managed in Scotland (which had about 10% of the total British population). One-third of

---

[70] Interview with Max Ward.

[71] The memorandum is titled 'Thoughts on Planning for the Future' and is undated. However, my copy was initialled and dated in handwriting by Richard Burns on 6 January 1987. The memorandum includes data from 1986 and I assume it was written either at the end of December 1986 or at the beginning of January 1987.

the latter sum was managed by the Scottish 'big three'; namely, Ivory & Sime, Baillie Gifford and Murray Johnstone.[72]

Progress in Total Funds under Management and Pension Funds

However, Scottish fund managers had not made as much progress in other investment vehicles such as pension funds and unit trusts. In early 1985, for example, it was reported that "Edinburgh's fund managers have been slow to get into the management of pension funds and the even-more-profitable unit trusts (mutual funds)".[73] At the end of 1984 financial institutions in Edinburgh accounted for only £387 million of the £15.9 billion of unit trusts managed from Britain (i.e. less than 2.5%).[74] Baillie Gifford itself had made significant progress as shown in Exhibit 4.2.

Exhibit 4.2. Baillie Gifford's funds under management, 1982-1988

Date	Total Funds under Management	Proportion in Investment Trusts (%)	Proportion in Pension Funds (%)
1982	£501 million [1]	£400 million [1] (80)	£100 million [1] (20)
1984	£900 million [2]	-	-
1988	£2,040 million [1]	-	£1,120 million [1] (55)

[1] *Financial Times*, 6 April 1988.
[2] *The Banker*, 1 April 1995.

[72] *The Economist*, 10 September 1983.
[73] *The Economist*, 16 February 1985.
[74] ibid.

Two observations emerge clearly from Exhibit 4.2. The first is the significant increase in total funds under management between 1982 and 1988, a four-fold increase (in money terms). The second is the rapid increase in the proportion of the firm's funds under management held in pension funds. While in 1982 only 20% of funds under management were in pension funds, by 1988 this had increased to 55%. Furthermore, this also translated into a growing market share in the UK's segregated pension fund market, as shown in Exhibit 4.3.

According to Gavin Gemmell, from 1985/86 "…we suddenly got many UK pension fund clients".[75] The contribution this made to Baillie Gifford's growth is clear from Exhibit 4.2. The question, however, is to explain this performance, both absolute performance (relative to Baillie Gifford's past performance) as well as relative performance (measured by market share in the Scottish and UK markets). When asked by the author in an interview to explain this performance, Gemmell's answer was that: "We began to present ourselves better as a relatively small specialist firm, well-organised, and with strong competencies in stock-picking".[76]

Exhibit 4.3. Baillie Gifford's share of the total UK segregated pension fund market, 1985-1992

Date	UK Market Share
1985	0.2%
1992	1.8%

Source: *Sunday Times*, 3 October 1993

Marketing Baillie Gifford's Competencies in the 1980s

As we have seen, it was in response to the 1977 crisis that Baillie Gifford staff began going out in earnest in order to drum up

---

[75] Interview with Gavin Gemmell.
[76] ibid.

additional clients. This process had the positive effect of making them aware of their strong competencies relative to other fund managers. However, this awareness still had to be sold to potential clients. And the task was made even more difficult by the fact that Baillie Gifford lacked a tradition of marketing itself, a legacy of the George Chiene period when the firm expected – and got – potential clients to approach it, rather than the other way round.

A key turning point occurred in 1985.[77] According to Gavin Gemmell, it was in this year that a team from Baillie Gifford made a presentation to a potential pension fund client with which the firm already had a good connection. Despite this, however, Baillie Gifford failed to get the mandate. This made Gemmell realise that the firm would have to sell itself better.

In response to this realisation, Baillie Gifford appointed Brian Malcolm, its first full-time executive responsible for marketing. Unlike most of the firm's other executives, who joined straight from university, Malcolm moved to Baillie Gifford after 17 years in the City of London. Peter Murray was a further marketing appointment, working full-time in mainstream UK pension funds.[78] The results were both quick and gratifying. While in 1985 Baillie Gifford gained only four new pension funds, in 1987 it gained 12.[79] This achievement led Gemmell to the realisation that: "We [had] paid insufficient attention to advice from John Chiene [George Chiene's nephew, given some time earlier] that one person full time on marketing is much better than 2 or 3 people part time".[80]

However, at the same time Gemmell was forced to acknowledge that although Baillie Gifford's marketing in the UK had improved substantially, "US marketing has been very limited and Rockwell was a stroke of luck unlikely to be repeated without effort".[81] As was shown earlier, it was only after Ross Lidstone took over US marketing on a full-time basis that Baillie Gifford made its effective entry into the US market.

---

[77] The information contained in this and the following paragraphs is based on an interview with Gavin Gemmell reported in the *Financial Times*, 6 April 1988.

[78] Gavin Gemmell, 'Thoughts on Planning', (1987?), pp.4-5.

[79] *Financial Times*, 6 April 1988.

[80] Gavin Gemmell, 'Thoughts on Planning', (1987?), pp.2-3.

[81] ibid, pp.4-5. See earlier for the discussion of Rockwell as Baillie Gifford's second US client.

In selling itself in the pension fund market Baillie Gifford was able to leverage its strong position in investment trusts. As Gavin Gemmell explained: "The size of our investment trust business gave Baillie Gifford credibility in pension funds in the mid-1980s. We said that although we are small in pensions, we manage large investment trusts. In the late-1980s Scottish Mortgage [the firm's largest investment trust] was worth about £300 million".[82] Once the first few pension fund mandates were signed, the success became cumulative: "A virtuous cycle sets in. Once you win [a few clients], consultants become keen to put you on their list because they want to add value for their clients".[83]

In this way, Baillie Gifford was able to make pension fund trustees and consultants aware of its competencies without having to spend an enormous amount. As Gemmell acknowledged, "There was not a massive budget for marketing".[84] As noted earlier, Ross Lidstone, who was in charge of marketing in the US, and James Anderson who did the same for Europe, both worked out of Edinburgh. In this way they were able to coordinate their efforts tightly with the rest of the Baillie Gifford staff.[85]

Japan as a Source of Clients

In 1963 Baillie Gifford began investing in Japanese financial assets, although the amount to begin with was fairly small.[86] In the 1970s the sum invested increased substantially but it was only around the mid-1970s that the firm began to make significant money from its Japanese investments.[87] In 1981 the Baillie Gifford Japan Trust was established.

The firm's competencies relating to Japanese financial assets would soon be richly rewarded when it turned out that potential clients in the US were particularly impressed with Baillie Gifford's

---

[82] Interview with Gavin Gemmell.

[83] ibid.

[84] ibid.

[85] The fund managing firm, Henderson, at the same time established a US office with a budget of around £2 million per annum. However, after two years it had gained no clients.

[86] Interview with Gavin Gemmell.

[87] Interview with Richard Burns.

skills in this area. [As noted earlier, it was in 1983 that Angus Millar and Gavin Gemmell first visited the US with a view to seeking US clients and engaged their first US client, the Republic Bank.] As Richard Burns noted: "Our involvement in Japan was a turning point for Baillie Gifford. It was one of the firm's key differenttiators in the US".[88] Gavin Gemmell adds: "We were perceived in the US as long-term, knowledgeable investors in Japan".[89] In 1985 Baillie Gifford Shin Nippon was established.

In 1980 Gavin Gemmell visited Japan in search of potential clients. As noted earlier, Japan featured as one of the six priorities listed in the Baillie Gifford business plan in the mid-1980s. More specifically, the firm undertook to: "Speak to any potential partners in managing Japanese money". Gemmell's visit bore fruit, even if it did take nine years. In 1989 Baillie Gifford agreed a joint venture with the Toyo Trust and Banking Company, with Baillie Gifford providing the fund management expertise. At that time, Toyo, part of the Sanwa Bank, had funds worth $63 billion and was the twenty-sixth largest banking institution in the world.[90]

To complete the story, after a process of merger and acquisition, Toyo became incorporated in the UFJ Trust, part of the giant UFJ financial group, which was Japan's fourth-largest banking group. The joint venture was re-named UFJ Baillie Gifford. On 25 April 2004 it was announced that Baillie Gifford had won the mandate to run the entire active portion of UFJ Trust's overseas equity portfolio. Baillie Gifford's "...contract with UFJ Trust...will be expanded to Yen 450 billion (£2.5 billion) and broadened to include North American equities in addition to European stocks".[91] In this way, UFJ became Baillie Gifford's

---

[88] ibid.

[89] Interview with Gavin Gemmell. Gemmell notes that US clients also wanted investments in European companies and this encouraged Baillie Gifford to increase its strength in this area too, leading in 1984 to the establishment of a European department.

[90] *Financial Times*, 8 December 1989. In 1987, Ivory & Sime, also based in Edinburgh, had concluded a joint venture with the Sumitomo financial group. Sumitomo became a major shareholder in Ivory & Sime and at one stage was even seen as a potential buyer of Ivory & Sime. In sharp contrast, Toyo had no ownership stake in Baillie Gifford, the firm retained its partnership status.

[91] *Financial Times*, 25 April 2004.

largest single client. By 2003, Baillie Gifford claimed to have the largest team of financial specialists working on Japanese investments outside Japan.[92]

The 1989 Succession

In April 1989 Angus Millar retired as the sole senior partner at the head of Baillie Gifford. However, Millar had left vague the question of succession. In the absence of commonly agreed rules of succession this meant that there was ambiguity regarding who would take over the leadership. In terms of age, experience and role played in the firm there were two obvious choices; Gavin Gemmell and Douglas McDougall. The problem was that both men had some expectation that they would succeed Angus Millar. In the words of one of the senior staff, "It was all rather awkward".

Until this time Baillie Gifford usually had one senior partner who acted as the head of the firm, in effect serving as a combined CEO and CIO (chief investment officer). The only exception was in the post-Second World War period when although Carlyle Gifford was the sole legal governing partner, owning all the firm's equity and stock, it was George Chiene who was *de facto* senior partner in charge of day-to-day activities. As Gifford got older, so more and more *de facto* power was devolved to Chiene.

After this time, "...there was a distinct pecking order [in Baillie Gifford]. The senior partner chaired all the meetings".[93] After Ernest Dawson retired in April 1975 and was replaced by Charles White there was some discussion of a division of labour at the top of the firm. However, in 1977 the Edinburgh and Dundee Investment Co crisis broke and nothing was done.

In 1988 the idea of a division of labour was resuscitated. On the one hand, a division of labour made good organisational sense in view of the growing responsibilities (requiring increasing amounts of information) of Baillie Gifford's top person as the size and complexity of the firm increased (including its growing number of clients). On the other hand, a division of labour between Gavin Gemmell and Douglas McDougall would also provide a

---

[92] *Investment Trusts*, Winter, 2003, p.50.
[93] Interview with Gavin Gemmell.

suitable way for both men to succeed Angus Millar, thus neatly side-stepping the potential for conflict over the succession issue.

In the end, discussion amongst the most senior of the partners resulted in agreement regarding a division of labour. Gavin Gemmell would become CEO, focusing on client development and business development more generally. Douglas McDougall would become CIO, dealing with Baillie Gifford's investments.[94] They would each chair the meetings that took place in their respective domains. According to one of the other senior members, "...although they are of very different temperament, they worked very well together", the skills of each complementing the other.

Gavin Gemmell

Gavin Gemmell was born on 7 September 1941 in Gullane, East Lothian. He was educated at George Watson's College, Edinburgh, and went on to become a chartered accountant. He joined Baillie Gifford in 1964. In 1967 he became a partner and in the same year he married. In 1973 he became the partner in charge of pension fund clients.

From 1983 he was a director of Baillie Gifford Overseas Limited and from 1985 a director of Baillie Gifford Shin Nippon plc. In 1984 he was appointed deputy chairman of Scottish Widows, later becoming chairman. He later became a director of Scottish Widows' parent company, Lloyds TSB. From 1990 he served as chairman of the Baillie Gifford Toyo Trust and from 1991 he was a director of Guardian Baillie Gifford.

In 2003 he was Chairman of Court at Heriot Watt University and a director of the Interactive University. He has been a trustee of the National Galleries of Scotland and is chairman of the Scottish Episcopal Church Standing Committee. Since retiring he has become involved in the business angel venture capital group, Archangel Informal Investments, and is a director of a number of small start-up companies. He is a member of the Scottish Enterprise Edinburgh & Lothian Board.[95] He was awarded the CBE in 1998.

---

[94] Interviews with Gavin Gemmell and Douglas McDougall.
[95] www.hanon.co.uk.

Douglas McDougall

Douglas Christopher Patrick McDougall was born on 18 March 1944. He was educated at the Edinburgh Academy and at Oxford University. In 1965, the year he graduated from Oxford, McDougall joined Baillie Gifford. He was made a partner in 1969. In June 1986 he married the daughter of Baron Griffiths, a law lord.

While at Baillie Gifford he served as non-executive director of Provincial Insurance plc (1989-94). From 1994-96 he was chairman of the Institutional Fund Managers Association and from 1995-98 he was chairman of the Association of Investment Trust Companies (AITC). He became chairman of the Investment Management Regulatory Organisation (IMRO) in July 1997 and held this position until 2000.

From 1998 McDougall was director of the Baillie Gifford Japan Trust. In October 2003 he was chairman of: the Law Debenture Corporation plc (joining the board in 1998 and becoming chairman in 2000), 3i Bioscience Investment Trust plc (appointed to the board in 1999), Foreign & Colonial Eurotrust plc, the Independent Investment Trust plc and Pacific Horizon Investment Trust plc.[96] He was also director of the Herald Investment Trust plc and the Monks Investment Trust plc. In October 2003 he succeeded the long-serving Sir Angus Grossart as the Chairman of the Scottish Investment Trust.[97] Since 1985 he has been a member of the Investment Committee at Cambridge University and from 1999 he was deputy chairman of Sand Aire Ltd. In 2001 he was awarded an OBE.

Some of Baillie Gifford's Scottish Competitors

In the early 1980s, as noted earlier, although Baillie Gifford was one of the top three independent Edinburgh fund managers, it was the smallest of the three and was perceived as being the laggard amongst them. The other two firms were Ivory & Sime and Martin

---

[96] Scottish Investment Trust web site.
[97] ibid.

Currie. At this time, according to Richard Burns, "Ivory and Sime looked excellent".[98]

By the early 1990s, however, some five years after the financial 'big bang' of UK deregulation that occurred in 1986, Baillie Gifford had improved its relative performance. In 1991, the firm became Scotland's number one manager of segregated pension funds, ousting Murray Johnstone from that position.[99] In 1992, Baillie Gifford took over the management of the Pacific Horizon Investment Trust (which had been established in 1989). In 1992, Baillie Gifford managed pension funds worth £2.25 billion.[100]

Exhibit 4.4 shows the growth in real funds under management (after taking account of inflation) for the five-year period from 1988 to 1993 for seven of the top Scottish fund managers.

Attempts by Several US Institutions to Acquire Baillie Gifford

However, in 1990 a number of US financial institutions visited Baillie Gifford with a view to negotiating its purchase. Nevertheless, these approaches were rejected by Baillie Gifford's partners, primarily because they did not want to lose their independence.[101] We will return later to the important implications of this rejection in a discussion of the firm's partnership mode of governance under the broader heading of 'Baillie Gifford's Culture'.

In the next few years Baillie Gifford made significant progress. In 1991 in the US Baillie Gifford agreed a joint venture with the Guardian Life Assurance Company of America. The initial agreement related to the management of an international fund aimed at US private investors.[102] In 2000, the partnership with

---

[98] Interview with Richard Burns.

[99] *Sunday Times*, 22 September 1991.

[100] Hymans Robertson survey, 1992. At this time, however, Scotland's top-ten pension fund managers managed only 6.2% of the total UK pension fund market, a result described as "derisory" by a Hymans Robertson senior partner.

[101] This information was made public by Gavin Gemmell in an interview quoted in the *Financial Times*, 8 February 1991.

[102] *Financial Times*, 8 February 1991.

Guardian Life added more than $1 billion, spread over four funds, to Baillie Gifford's funds under management.[103]

Exhibit 4.4. Edinburgh investment managers: growth in real funds under management, 1988-1993

Fund Manager	Growth, 1988-1993 (per annum)
Edinburgh Fund Managers	+ 18%
Baillie Gifford	+ 17%
Stewart Ivory	- 11%
Martin Currie	- 12%
Ivory & Sime	- 13%
Murray Johnstone	- 15%
Dunedin	- 24%

Source: *Sunday Times*, 3 October 1993.

In 1992 Baillie Gifford was chosen for the £420 million mandate to manage stock market investments for Provincial Insurance. The previous year Baillie Gifford had won the company's pension fund. This made the Provincial contract the biggest block of money managed by Baillie Gifford after Scottish Mortgage.[104]

However, 1993 "…was a very bad year for Baillie Gifford. We got the ERM [European Exchange Rate Mechanism] wrong. We thought that the UK would stay in the ERM. So we did badly".[105] Unfortunately for the firm, the poor performance, particularly in UK equities, continued into 1996. Max Ward recalls

---

[103] *Business a.m.*, 27 September 2000.
[104] *Financial Times*, 15 May 1992.
[105] Interview with Richard Burns.

these as "...dark days – very stressful".[106] Nevertheless, in 1997 the firm's fortunes changed dramatically. During the years 1997 to 1999, according to Ward, Baillie Gifford recorded "...fantastic performance".[107]

Takeover of Dunedin

By 1996 it was clear that Dunedin, in view of its poor performance, was ripe for takeover. Although generally reluctant to engage in acquisitions, Baillie Gifford showed some interest in Dunedin. As Gavin Gemmell later recalled: "We have looked [for acquisitions] from time to time. [For example,] Dunedin came up. We had a look at it. We felt it was worth about half what the eventual buyer decided. Acquisitions is a particular skill we don't really have".[108] Ultimately, it was Edinburgh Fund Managers that acquired Dunedin.

Globalisation – Germany

In 1998 Baillie Gifford entered the German market through an alliance with Mannheimer, a general insurance company based in Mannheim. The initial agreement involved giving equity advice to the German company.[109] According to Gavin Gemmell, the contract with Mannheimer followed directly from the recruitment of Bill Richards, who had previously worked for Deutsche Bank's asset management arm.[110]

The 1999 Succession

In April 1999 Douglas McDougall retired as senior partner and it was known that Gavin Gemmell would retire two years later. Richard Burns succeeded Douglas McDougall in his CIO role,

---

[106] Interview with Max Ward.
[107] ibid.
[108] *The Herald*, 8 February 2001.
[109] *Financial Times*, 11 December 1998.
[110] Gavin Gemmell, quoted in *Financial News*, 14 December 1998.

while Alex Callander took over Gemmell's responsibilities as CEO in 2001.

Richard Burns

Richard Burns was born on 5 May 1946. He joined Baillie Gifford in 1973 after working for 18 months as a solicitor. He was educated at Trinity College, Glenalmond. He read history at Merton College, Oxford, followed by law at the University of Edinburgh. He became a Writer to the Signet (WS) on 24 April 1972 after serving his apprenticeship under Charles Annand Fraser and others at W. & J. Burness. In 1977 he became a partner and began work with Gavin Gemmell on developing the pension fund department. He managed Mid Wynd International Investment Trust from its stock market debut in 1981 to 1991. He has been on its board since 1981. In 1989 he became head of the Institutional Clients Department. In April 1999 he also took over as head of the firm's four-person investment policy committee. At the same time he became manager of the Monks Investment Trust. He joined the board of Baillie Gifford Japan Trust in May 2001.

Alex Callander

He was born on 1 April 1960 and read mathematics at Cambridge University. He joined Baillie Gifford after graduating. He first worked as an oil analyst for Douglas McDougall. Subsequently he became manager of the Winterbottom Energy Trust. After it was taken over, he joined Gemmell and Burns in the Institutional Clients Department.

Growth despite the 2000 Stock Market Bust

From 2000, new mandates came pouring in. In the course of 2000 Baillie Gifford took in around £2.5 billion of new business. This included £1 billion from ten UK institutional clients, including the £440 million Post Office Pension Fund. From the US came mandates worth approximately £1 billion, including £300 million from the New York Teachers' Pension fund.[111]

In 2001, a difficult time for most investment managers, Baillie Gifford won £1.4 billion of new business, even though for much of the year the company did not accept new pension mandates. Clients during this year included Calpers, the world's largest pension fund based in California.[112]

A breakdown of Baillie Gifford's funds under management, according to type of fund, for the years 1993, 1995 and 2001 is shown in Exhibit 4.5.

Exhibit 4.5. Breakdown of Baillie Gifford's funds under management, 1993, 1995, and 2001

Fund Type	1993 Value, £bn (number)	1995 Value, £bn (number)	2001 Value, £bn (number)
Pension Funds	£4.4 (85)	£7.0 (79)	£14.1 (115)
Investment Trusts	£1.7 (7)	£1.8 (6)	£2.8 (6)
Unit Trusts, Offshore Funds, OEICs	£0.4 (15)	£0.7 (20)	£0.2 (17)
Insurance Funds	£0.8 (7)	£0.9 (7)	£0.5 (3)
Other (overseas funds, charities)	£0.6 (20)	£0.9 (44)	£4.4 (57)
Total	**£7.9**	**£11.2**	**£21.9**

Source: Adapted from CA Magazine, *Who's Who in Fund Management*, 1993, 1995, 2001.

---

[111] *Business a.m.*, 29 November 2000.
[112] *Business a.m.*, 19 November 2001.

In 2002, when the FTSE-100 hit a seven-year low, Baillie Gifford received £2.5 billion of new business, at a time when "…many other fund managers were having a horrible time". The mandates included West Sussex County Council Superannuation fund, worth £360 million, the US firm Caterpillar and Scottish & Newcastle, each valued at about £100 million.[113] In the same year, Baillie Gifford received a mandate in Sweden to manage half of the £100 million pension fund for the Swedish construction group, Skanska.[114]

However, not everything went Baillie Gifford's way in 2002. In this year the firm made a bid for the management contract for the Edinburgh Investment Trust that had been held by Edinburgh Fund Managers since the latter's takeover of Dunedin in 1996. Although several commentators felt that Baillie Gifford was the most likely replacement, in the event the contract went to Fidelity, moving the management of this trust south of the border for the first time in over 100 years.[115]

By 2003 Baillie Gifford had made its mark globally in the pension fund market, as shown in Exhibit 4.6. North American clients included Calpers, the world's largest pension fund, the New York State retirement fund, the City of Montreal pension fund, Goodyear, J.C. Penney and United Airlines.

In 2003, Baillie Gifford took over from Edinburgh Fund Managers the contract to manage the £112 million Edinburgh Worldwide Investment Trust.[116] Towards the end of the year, Baillie Gifford was awarded the management contract for the Scottish American Investment Trust Company (SAINTS) that had previously been managed by First State Investments.[117] SAINTS was the first investment trust company to be launched in Edinburgh in April 1873 as discussed earlier. It was masterminded by William John Menzies whose visits to the US in 1864, 1867 and 1872 convinced him of the investment opportunities which existed in that country. The first Scottish investment trust had been

[113] *The Herald*, 24 January 2003.
[114] *Financial Times*, 11 February 2002.
[115] *The Herald*, 10 July 2002.
[116] *The Scotsman*, 3 September 2003.
[117] *The Scotsman*, 10 December 2003.

established by Robert Fleming in Dundee two months earlier in February 1873 and was called the Scottish American Investment Trust.[118] However, Baillie Gifford lost out to Standard Life in the competition to take over the management of the Edinburgh Small Companies Trust, formerly run by Edinburgh Fund Managers.[119]

Exhibit 4.6. Indicators of Baillie Gifford's strength in the global pension fund market, 2003

- Baillie Gifford's clients include 5 of the world's 15 largest pension funds

- In the US Baillie Gifford has mandates from 4 of the largest 8 US pension funds

- In each of the world's three main economic regions – North America, Europe and Japan – Baillie Gifford manages funds for at least one of the top 3 pension funds in the region

Source: *Financial Times*, 6 January 2003; *Sunday Herald*, 24 August 2003 and 23 November 2003.

By 2004 it was clear that Baillie Gifford was one of Scotland's major success stories, as can be seen from the data provided in Exhibit 4.7.

---

[118] Newlands (1997), pp.57 and 74.
[119] *The Herald*, 14 August 2003 and *The Scotsman*, 3 September 2003.

Exhibit 4.7. Indicators of Baillie Gifford's development

Indicator	
International Activities	1989 – 1999: funds managed from outside the UK expand by a factor of 50 [1] By end-2003 overseas funds (i.e. non-UK) constitute 30% of total funds under management [2]
Employment	1986: 100 [1] 2002: 420 [1]
Number of Partners	1982: 8 [3] 1995: 15 [4] 2004: 27 [5]
Size	In 2004 Baillie Gifford was by far the largest independent fund management firm in the UK structured as a partnership [5]

Source: [1] *CA Magazine*, August 2002; [2] www.bailliegifford.com; [3] Baillie Gifford; [4] *CA Magazine*, December 1995; [5] Baillie Gifford Press Release, 19 January 2004.

BAILLIE GIFFORD'S CULTURE

Firm Culture

It has sometimes been suggested that the difference in behaviour and performance of firms operating within essentially the same environment is due to firm 'culture'. However, this proposal is problematical. The reason, simply, is that far from providing a sufficient explanation of behaviour and performance, culture itself needs to be explained. As in the case of countries, company culture is not static but changes over time. It is therefore necessary to explain why culture takes the form that it does at any point in time and why it changes the way it does over time. Furthermore, the term culture is usually used to refer to a complex aggregation of factors that, it is hypothesised, influence behaviour and performance. To avoid culture becoming a catch-all that ends up confusing more than it illuminates it is necessary to unbundle the concept in order to focus on the individual causal components.

What Makes Baillie Gifford Different?

Baillie Gifford partners are likely to agree with Douglas McDougall who, in an interview with the author, suggested there are three key interrelated features of the firm's culture: academic rigour; a sense of professional service; and the partnership mode of governance. Put together these three features, McDougall argued, are responsible for making Baillie Gifford a "...strong firm personality".[120] Each of these factors will be examined in detail.

Academic rigour
There is a widespread perception that Baillie Gifford is an 'academic' and 'intellectual' firm. In 1987, for example, *The Economist* stated that within the Scottish investment community: "Baillie Gifford is the most academic of the houses".[121] In 1988 the

---

[120] Interview with Douglas McDougall.
[121] *The Economist*, 19 December 1987.

Financial Times referred to: "Baillie Gifford's detached, rather intellectual approach to life".[122]

There is a correspondence between this external perception and the history of Baillie Gifford. Douglas McDougall is in no doubt that the firm's academic rigour "...come from Carlyle Gifford and Charles White" (whose attitudes were discussed earlier in this chapter[123]).[124] According to McDougall, before many other UK investment managers, "...we were doing our own rigorous research as opposed to just listening to stockbrokers and investment bankers".[125]

The priority attached to academic rigour has been deeply engrained in Baillie Gifford's recruitment routines. In discussing the importance of this issue Douglas McDougall reflected, "We were like the Jesuits (you can quote me on that)".[126] He elaborated: "We wanted to recruit young people straight from university who would come to share our values and beliefs".[127] McDougall did all the recruiting for Baillie Gifford for about 30 years: "We brought in all our people from university and went each year to Oxford and Cambridge to recruit – most of our top people came from Oxford. This gave an academic reputation to Baillie Gifford".[128]

But, as is well-acknowledged, 'academic' can also be a pejorative term, particularly in a business environment, connoting a lack of contact with the real world. In Baillie Gifford's case, however, favoured recruitment from good universities went together with a rigorous process of further in-house training. According to Max Ward, "...almost all our people were taught how to invest in Baillie Gifford".[129] In 1991, for example, 90% of

---

[122] *Financial Times*, 6 April 1988.
[123] See, for example, Charles White's own account of Carlyle Gifford's academic attitudes and the role that they played in his (White's) own appointment, discussed earlier.
[124] Interview with Douglas McDougall.
[125] ibid.
[126] ibid.
[127] ibid.
[128] ibid.
[129] Interview with Max Ward.

Baillie Gifford's then 35 "...investment professionals" were trained in the firm.[130]

Rigorous in-house training has produced two important benefits. The first of these is an understanding of the processes – organisational, informational and technical – necessary to master the task of investment, drawing on the knowledge and experience that Baillie Gifford has accumulated over the years. This knowledge and experience is passed on inter-generationally through the in-house training procedure.

The second benefit of in-house training is just as important. In Max Ward's words, in-house training meant "...we all understood where each other was coming from".[131] In turn, this shared perspective produces further second-round benefits. Most importantly, it helps to create the conditions for the effective co-operation of the firm's various teams. With a common background and many shared fundamental assumptions effective co-operation is more likely to take place (though, of course, it is by no means guaranteed).

But surely shared assumptions and a common background also have a downside since they may lead to blind-spots, complacence and biases? While this must be true, it is here that the academic-oriented attitudes of Baillie Gifford staff provide some degree of protection. One of the fundamentals of a sound academic education is the ability to look critically at the world, including the internal world of the firm which provides an employment home. It seems that Baillie Gifford provides an environment where critical debate is not only encouraged but also required. The firm's habitual distrust of 'investment stars' in favour of broad-based, co-operative decision-making reinforces this environment.

A sense of professional service

Douglas McDougall is in no doubt that Baillie Gifford's commitment to high standards of client service is a key element in the firm's historical heritage. Indeed, it is a commitment that goes back to the days of George Chiene, if not before: "George Chiene was anti-growth but believed in high standards of service – putting

---

[130] *Sunday Times*, 22 September 1991.
[131] Interview with Max Ward.

clients first; commitment and loyalty to clients. He was a man of fantastic morals".[132]

Of course, all companies claim to be fully committed to the well-being of their customers, even if in practice this turns out to be a 'motherhood and apple pie'-type claim. However, there does appear to be some evidence to justify the claim that Baillie Gifford is prepared to go further than most in the interests of their clients. One example is the firm's practice of closing its books to new customers when it is felt that the growth in clients has begun to stretch resources. As Gavin Gemmell explained in October 1993 after Baillie Gifford had closed its books: "We limit our expansion to prudent targets set at the start of each year, even if that means turning business away".[133] During 2000 the firm temporarily suspended further contracts for segregated pension fund management, the third time in a decade that it had done so.

But what do Baillie Gifford's clients make of this practice; do they have the same perspective on it as the firm does? Lacking a proper survey of clients it is not possible to answer this question with certainty. However, some clients have publicly expressed their views. One example is Ray Martinhead of the Scottish & Newcastle pension fund who explained his fund's involvement with Baillie Gifford: "We were attracted to these smaller houses, because we were confident that their processes won't change. They are not focused on just growing assets and will close their books when they get too big, so ensuring existing clients won't suffer".[134] In the second half of 2001 Baillie Gifford again closed its books and in 2003 it temporarily suspended its emerging markets products.[135]

Partnership structure

According to Douglas McDougall, Baillie Gifford's partnership structure is not only crucial in its own right but is also "…the key to [reproducing] our first two beliefs", that is academic rigour and professional service. Since partnership is a major

---

[132] Interview with Douglas McDougall.

[133] Quoted in *Sunday Times*, 3 October 1993.

[134] *Global Investor*, December 2002/January 2003.

[135] *The Sunday Herald*, 24 August 2003.

feature of Baillie Gifford's corporate organisation its implications will be closely analysed in this section.

Many financial institutions involved in investing in new and existing financial assets, both in the UK and US, began as partnerships. The claim has frequently been made that partnership is a superior mode of governance for an investment management firm compared to the alternatives that exist. More specifically, it has been argued that partnership may produce superior performance in the longer term. However, notwithstanding these arguments, over time in the UK and US partnerships have tended to give way to other alternative modes of governance. This raises an evolutionary puzzle; if partnership is a 'fitter' form of organisation, why has it tended to be squeezed out in the evolutionary process? The history of Baillie Gifford throws some light on this intriguing question.[136]

Joseph Stiglitz, Nobel Prize-winning economist, has expressed some of the dilemmas surrounding this question:

"The event which perhaps captured – some may say epitomized – the new mood of the banks [in the 'Roaring Nineties'] was the decision of Goldman Sachs, one of the most prestigious of the investment banks...to go public. Most of the investment banks had been founded as partnerships. Now, one after another, they decided to cash in and become incorporated. Goldman Sachs took the plunge on May 4, 1999. Incorporation allowed Goldman to be listed on the New York Stock Exchange, and to participate in the bull market. But at the same time, it protected Goldman's executives against downside risk. As a partner, each had been liable for the mistakes, and the resulting financial loss, of the others. That made them strongly motivated to monitor each other's actions, which provided strong comfort to investors, but it was a task that was becoming increasingly difficult as the banks grew in size. Incorporation lifted that burden of responsibility from their shoulders, and offered the partners the

---

[136] The same may have been said of Standard Life, although this comparison will not be pursued here.

opportunity to take advantage of soaring stock prices and make a short-term killing. Economic theory would predict that such moves by the banks would lead to greater risk taking, a greater focus on the short run, and this indeed seems to have been the case".[137]

Stiglitz argues that prior to the 'Roaring Nineties' US investment banks played a major role in monitoring the performance of the management of companies and disciplining the management if need be. This was a role that could not be played effectively by the millions of shareholders who held the shares in these companies. Although managers were supposed to advance the interests of their shareholders: "…in truth, they often advanced their own interests, at the expense of the average shareholder; the stock options and other devices that made it difficult for ordinary shareholders to see what was really going on only made matters worse".[138] The monitoring and disciplining role of the investment banks was therefore crucial. However, Stiglitz suggests, the erosion of the partnership mode of governance of the investment banks and their incorporation led to these banks becoming caught up in the excesses of the bull market and resulted in the undermining of their crucial role, to the detriment of the entire US economy.

The partnership mode of governance has always been the foundation of Baillie Gifford ever since the founding of the firm in 1907, as was shown earlier in this book, when Augustus Baillie took Carlyle Gifford on as his younger partner. While it is true that the partnership ship at times sailed into rough waters – the crisis conflict between Carlyle Gifford and George Chiene after the Second World War being a case in point – it remains the case that this mode of governance generally provided a solid foundation for the firm's activities and for co-operation between its partners.

But since, as Stiglitz has noted, partners have frequently decided to terminate their partnerships, it is necessary to ask why

---

[137] Stiglitz, J. 2003. *The Roaring Nineties: Seeds of Destruction*. London: Allen Lane, pp.147-8.
[138] ibid, p.146.

Baillie Gifford's partners have not decided to follow suit. In short, why has the partnership continued to exist?

Douglas McDougall provides part of the answer when he observes, "We have a strong sense of it being our firm".[139] However, Alex Callander, current joint senior partner with Richard Burns, takes this one step further when he says: "I am sure the vast majority of us believe that we basically hold this business in trust and there is no wish to sell".[140]

The notion of 'holding Baillie Gifford in trust' is particularly intriguing and requires further comment. For whom is the firm being held in trust? The only possible answer to this question is that the firm is being held in trust for current and future partners. This answer is of particular interest because it implies a sense of both loyalty and obligation to the current and future partners who will carry on the line of this almost-family-firm, the partners constituting the family members. In short, to the extent that Callander's observations reflect the general feeling among the partners, there is a broader commitment to the firm and its future as a partnership that extends beyond narrow short-term self-interest.

But what about self-interest? Has it simply been subordinated by the partners to a strong belief in the greater future good? Douglas McDougall provides an illuminating answer to these questions when he notes that: "We didn't cash out [by incorporating Baillie Gifford]. This contributed to a personality that has won business".[141] However, McDougall's two sentences must be taken separately. First, why did Baillie Gifford's partners decide not to cash out? Secondly, what are the consequences of maintaining the firm's partnership mode of governance?

The first question is of more than theoretical interest since, as noted earlier, in 1990 a number of US institutions visited Baillie Gifford with a view to negotiating its purchase.[142] In the event, the partners rejected these overtures. But why did they not opt to cash out, given the rich rewards that were likely to follow (in 1990, or

---

[139] Interview with Douglas McDougall.
[140] Quoted in *The Sunday Herald*, 24 August 2003.
[141] Interview with Douglas McDougall.
[142] Gavin Gemmell quoted in the *Financial Times*, 8 February 2001.

even more so, towards the end of the decade)? It seems there are several likely components to the answer to this question.

To begin with, it is probably true that in the short term at least cashing out would have left the partners significantly better off financially than the alternative of maintaining their partnership. However, against this had to be weighed a number of disadvantages of the cash out option.

First, cashing out also implies subordination to external owners (e.g. a financial conglomerate and shareholders). This means an increase in external pressure and a corresponding diminution of independence. Baillie Gifford's partners value their independence.[143] Secondly, although cashing out might bring short-term financial gain, it ran the risk of eliminating one of Baillie Gifford's main claims to distinctiveness, namely the partnership structure itself, which, the firm argues, promotes longer-term performance advantages. Accordingly, to the extent that cashing out reduced the firm's attractiveness in the eyes of its clients, it may have reduced the firm's profitability. Thirdly, and perhaps most importantly, the partners realised that the partnership mode of governance had served them and the firm well in the past and had been compatible with relatively good remuneration, and that there was therefore no compelling reason to give it up.[144]

This brings us to Douglas McDougall's second sentence. Not cashing out, he says, "…contributed to a personality that has won business". But what are the benefits of the 'partnership personality'?

---

[143] According to Richard Burns: "One organisation tried to take us over. The price was right. But the partnership objected to losing their independence". Interview with Richard Burns.

[144] The quotation above from Stiglitz suggests a further reason why Baillie Gifford's partners, unlike their US investment bank counterparts, decided to retain their partnership mode of governance. In the US case, Stiglitz argues, the size of investment banks began to compromise the ability of partners to monitor the activities of their fellow partners. This removed one of the main benefits of the partnership mode of governance. In Baillie Gifford's case, in contrast, arguably size has not yet impinged on the firm's ability to reap the governance advantages of partnership. Furthermore, partnership continues to contribute significantly to a sense of shared community and loyalty which in turn have facilitated effective co-operation.

At least three sets of benefits deriving from the partnership mode of governance may be distinguished. The first deals with the effect of partnership on the values, attitudes and beliefs of the partners themselves. The second has to do with the impact of partnership on the investment process, while the third involves the consequences regarding the responses of clients. It is worth separating these three sets of effects.

Alex Callander has summarised the first set of benefits, namely the effect of the partnership mode of governance on the partners themselves: "Partnership enables people to be reasonably secure in their positions, therefore they're much more willing to say what they think rather than what they think they ought to say, so we keep the politics down and ensure a high level of intellectual debate".[145] Callander elaborates: "The senior people own the business and the middle ranking people hope to own the business. This means that if you see something that you don't quite like, your first reaction is to try and improve it rather than to go off and get a job elsewhere".[146] This first set of benefits clearly reinforces one feature of the 'Baillie Gifford Culture', namely academic rigour, that has already been discussed.

Richard Burns notes one of the major benefits that partnership has for the investment process: "Being private allows you to drive the business at the speed which suits the clients".[147] He gives as an example the several occasions (referred to above) on which Baillie Gifford has turned down additional funds. It would normally not be easy for a quoted company to justify this kind of decision to its shareholders. More generally, as Alex Callander notes: "We can afford to take a longer-term view because we don't have outside shareholders hammering the table and asking about quarterly profit figures".[148] These benefits strengthen Baillie Gifford's sense of professional service, the second feature of the firm's culture.

---

[145] Quoted in *The Herald*, 19 April 2003.
[146] Quoted in *The Sunday Herald*, 24 August 2003. Or, in the words of Albert Hirschmann, the partnership mode of governance encourages the use of voice and loyalty rather than exit. See Hirschmann, A.O. (1970).
[147] Richard Burns, quoted in the *Financial Times*, 6 January 2003.
[148] *The Herald*, 19 April 2003.

It is likely that clients also see significant benefits flowing from Baillie Gifford's partnership mode of governance. One important benefit is the continuity and stability in the relationship between the firm and its clients. As Douglas McDougall noted: "I know of no other firm where so many senior people have never worked anywhere else".[149] This continuity and stability helps to produce two of the most important ingredients in the investor-client relationship; trust and confidence. In a world where uncertainty makes it impossible to predict performance – of individual shares, groups of shares and of investment managers – trust and confidence become a key driver of choice of fund manager. It seems clear that Baillie Gifford's partnership structure has helped the firm to inculcate a sense of confidence and trust on the part of its clients.

However, one key way in which the trust and confidence of clients is established and maintained is through the personal unlimited liability of the partners. This liability sends an important signal to clients, telling them that to some extent the risk they are taking is shared by their investment managers. These managers in turn, as Stiglitz notes, have an incentive to monitor each other's actions, thus reducing the chances of moral hazard.

Douglas McDougall summarises the feelings of Baillie Gifford's partners when he argues that: "Ideally, ownership and management should be the same".[150] It is precisely the *separation* of ownership and management that many economists have argued, though necessary, has led to a significant conflict of interest in the modern corporation. This conflict has been referred to as the 'principal-agent problem' and a good deal of attention has been paid to ways of overcoming the problem through the creation of appropriate incentives so that agents will act in the interest of their principals. However, the *unity* of ownership and management inherent in Baillie Gifford's partnership structure, as McDougall suggests, solves the problem by sidestepping it.

Nevertheless, the present discussion of the benefits of partnership does, as noted at the outset of this section, raise a broader puzzle. If partnership is such a 'fit' form of organisation, why has

---

[149] Interview with Douglas McDougall.
[150] ibid.

it tended to give way to other forms of governance? In short, why is Baillie Gifford something of an exception in this regard?

The answers to these questions are also inherent in the present discussion. Stiglitz has pointed to one of the answers when he notes that in the 1990s many of the leading US investment banks made the decision to incorporate and cash out rather than keep their partnership structure. The reason, he suggests, was two-fold. First, these firms had grown too large for the partnership mode of governance to play the function of self-monitoring by the partners. Secondly, he implies that the incentives for gain provided by the stock market boom of the late-1990s provided an additional reason for abandoning the partnership structure, thus allowing the investment banks and their senior staff to benefit both from the rising share value of their clients as well as their own share value. This combination of reasons was sufficient to overwhelm the benefits of partnership.

But in other cases where partnership has been abandoned, size may not have played a significant role. One example may be other Scottish fund managing firms who, though approximately the same size or even smaller than Baillie Gifford, chose to relinquish their partnership structures. In these cases it may be that only Stiglitz's second reason for the abandonment of partnership holds. Furthermore, the firms concerned may not have had as positive an experience with the partnership structure as did Baillie Gifford. It remains for further research to reveal whether their form of partnership differed in significant respects from that of Baillie Gifford.

Finally, a word of caution is needed to round off this discussion of partnership and not get too carried away by the benefits, ignoring some of its drawbacks. This comes from Richard Burns who, when pushed by the author to identify the possible disadvantages of partnership, commented: "There must be disadvantages. I suppose over-caution and slow-moving may be two of them".[151]

---

[151]   Interview with Richard Burns.

5

STANDARD LIFE INVESTMENTS, 1825-2004[1]

INTRODUCTION

Standard Life was Europe's largest mutual life insurance company. It is also Edinburgh's largest manager of funds. In this section the story of Standard Life's origins and development is told.

Origins

Standard Life was established on 23 March 1825 as the separate branch of a fire insurance company that had been set up in Edinburgh four years earlier.[2] The political machinations of

---

[1] This section draws heavily on the official history of Standard Life. Moss, M. 2000. *Standard Life, 1825-2000: The Building of Europe's Largest Mutual Life Company*. Edinburgh and London: Mainstream Publishing.

[2] Scottish Widows, one of the largest Edinburgh life insurance companies, had been established earlier in 1815. Both Scottish Widows and Standard Life were relative latecomers to the field of life insurance. Indeed, life insurance seems to have emerged from the prior area of marine insurance which provided some of the earliest examples of insurance in general and itself came out of the growing magnitude and importance of international trade. The earliest life insurance contract known "...was taken out by the Datini Company of Barcelona on 19 September 1399 on the life of Filipozo Soldani during a voyage from Barcelona to Italy". The earliest British life policy was dated 18 June 1583. [Lewin (2003), pp.112-3.] The first British institution to offer long-term life contracts to the public was the Mercers' Company in 1699 (ibid, p.325). The scientific underpinnings of the insurance industry had also emerged much earlier. In 1693 Edmond Halley published the first life table that showed how to value life annuities correctly, thus giving birth to actuarial science. This allowed the price for pensions and life assurance to be calculated. However, it took a long time before this scientific work had a noticeable impact on the activities of

Scotland at the time provided the soil from which Standard Life emerged. For many years Scotland's political life had been dominated by the Tories under the control of the Dundas family. At the time of Standard Life's establishment there was a tiny electorate numbering some 4,500 voters in the whole of Scotland. The Dundas family controlled not only the politics of the country but also much of its financial institutions.

In their struggle with the Tories, the Whigs pursued two strategies. The first was to support a significant extension of the franchise, in this way to loosen the political grip of the Tories. The second was to assist the formation of financial institutions that would compete with the dominant Tory-controlled institutions. In 1810 the Commercial Bank of Scotland was established in furtherance of this objective. And in 1821 an associated company was set up, the Insurance Company of Scotland which offered fire insurance. It was this company that four years later established the related company selling life insurance that would become Standard Life. The Duke of Hamilton became the first governor of the Insurance Company of Scotland and the Earl of Rosebery and Lord Blantyre his two deputy governors. All three men were leading Scottish Whigs.[3]

From the outset, Standard Life hoped to win custom from the emergent industrialists who were benefiting from the industrial revolution in areas such as textiles, metal-working and engineering. It was these industrialists who had much to gain from political reform that would give them a greater amount of influence.

---

the large number of life assurance companies that were established between 1680 and 1720. The unscientific basis of many of the companies' policies took its toll and a large number of them failed. It was only in 1848 that the UK's first professional association of actuaries was established. (Lewin (2003), pp.xii-xiii).

[3] In 1823 Tory sympathisers had established the Edinburgh Life Assurance Company and in 1824 the Tory Lord Provost of Edinburgh, Alexander Henderson, had floated the Scottish Union Insurance Company, a fire and life office.

Standard Life's Original Customers

As with the other life assurance companies at the time, Standard Life's main customers came from the aristocratic and landed class. Agricultural improvement on their large estates, made profitable by the impact of industrial revolution innovative advances on agriculture, frequently required substantial borrowing. Banks, legal practices and insurance companies provided many of these loans. Indeed, loans and life policies developed synergistically. Common practice was for large loans to be given only on condition that the borrower simultaneously took out a life policy to deal with the risk of default that might follow premature death.

But landed families also demanded life policies for other reasons. These included the complicated legal provisions recommended by prudent lawyers that often accompanied marriage intended to ensure future financial security. Products that were originally designed for the landed gentry were subsequently adapted to the needs of families involved in commerce and industry.

Since Edinburgh tended to be the Scottish city with the most influential and wealthy social and political networks in which nobles and landed families played a prominent role, it followed that financial institutions catering initially to their needs would quickly take root in this city. These institutions included not only banks and insurance companies but also professional services such as those provided by lawyers and accountants, many of whom went on to offer investment management services. Not only could life assurance companies help establish commercial and industrial companies through their loans, thereby facilitating entry and competition, they could also assist in their exit. This happened, for example, when the life of a bankrupt person was insured by his creditors, perhaps because the assets he owned could not be easily realised. Indeed, after the famous Scottish novelist, Sir Walter Scott, failed financially in 1826 he was heavily insured by his creditors.[4]

Although during the 1820s and '30s the majority of very large life policies were taken out by members of the aristocracy and

---

[4] Moss (2000), p.20.

landed gentry, increasingly smaller loans were extended for purposes that included the establishment or extension of small and medium-sized businesses. In 1828, for instance, Standard Life's policy holders (whose agreements linked loans to life policies) included a cotton spinner in Lancashire, an Edinburgh bookseller (William Chambers who founded the Chambers Dictionary) and an Edinburgh cabinet maker.[5] In this way Standard Life performed much the same function as today's venture capitalists.

Furthermore, the company soon committed itself to benefiting from the 'second' industrial revolution generated by the steam engine and railways. Targeting the English industrial market, a group of directors visited London and the English industrial districts in 1838. Shortly thereafter offices were opened in Manchester and Liverpool and local boards were appointed. Clearly, Standard Life's customer base had moved far from the Scottish nobility and landed gentry that the company began serving.

Drawing on the Knowledge of Edinburgh

Mathematics

The entry of the fledgling Standard Life into the life assurance market was helped by the knowledge available in Edinburgh. The original board of Standard Life included a Solicitor of the Supreme Court, two advocates, a merchant and a farmer. Amongst those soon added was Professor William Wallace, a Professor of Mathematics at the University of Edinburgh. Wallace was added because it was believed that his "…scientific knowledge might be highly beneficial to the Institution".[6] He was head-hunted from the board of Country Fire and Provident Life where he had learned a great deal about the calculation of life assurance risk and expected returns on investment in annuities. [At the time mortality rates were estimated on the basis of a study of death rates in Northampton from 1735-80 that had been undertaken for the Equitable insurance company. However, this data underestimated the life span of Standard Life's typical customer who was wealthy

---

[5] ibid, p.28.
[6] Quoted in Moss (2000), p.21.

and tended to live much longer. In 1826, the mathematician Charles Babbage (often regarded as the inventor of the computer) had complained about the 'immense' returns that insurance companies received by overestimating the premiums due on young people's lives. Wallace recommended that Standard Life's calculation be based on the tables used by Scottish Widows that made use of the Northampton data.]

Medicine

Use was also made by Standard Life and the other Edinburgh insurance companies of complementary knowledge located in Edinburgh. Particularly important were the Edinburgh physicians and surgeons who were appointed as referees for insurance proposals. Without them it would not have been possible to evaluate the risk involved in insuring specific individuals' lives.

By the time Standard Life was established, the University of Edinburgh had become as famous for its colleges and medical school as it was for philosophy (through the work of Enlightenment notables such as David Hume and Adam Smith). In 1681 the Royal College of Physicians of Edinburgh was established and in 1685 three titular Professors of Medicine were appointed, although none of them gave lectures and their appointments were not particularly productive. The surgeons of Edinburgh were formally organised from a far earlier period. In 1505 they were organised into a craft organisation, the Incorporation of Barber Surgeons, that had a close relationship with the Edinburgh Town Council. In 1697 a special building was erected, Old Surgeons' Hall (in what is now the University's High School Yards), for the purpose of anatomical demonstrations. This building was used by Edinburgh surgeons until 1725. In 1778 they were granted a royal charter as the Royal College of Surgeons of Edinburgh.

In 1720 the first Alexander Monro, Professor of Anatomy at the University, began giving anatomy lectures in Old Surgeons' Hall. Monro had studied at the famous medical school in Leyden in the Netherlands under Herman Boerhaave and this cemented an important link between the two centres with a number of Dutch professors of medicine coming to teach at the University of Edinburgh. However, the main breakthrough in the fortunes of medicine in Edinburgh occurred in 1726 when the Provost of

Edinburgh, George Drummond (who was also behind the establishment of Edinburgh's New Town), facilitated the setting up of a new medical school at the university. In 1729 Provost Drummond together with Alexander Monro established Edinburgh's Infirmary. This was a national charitable institution (not run by the Town Council) accepting patients from all over the country and financed by subscriptions. Monro and members of his family went on to establish what was referred to as the 'Monro dynasty' which played an important role in the development of the university's medical school. The first Alexander Monro remained Professor of Anatomy until 1759.[7]

The reputation of the University of Edinburgh's medical school was such that Charles Darwin's father decided to send him there to train as a doctor. Indeed, Charles entered the university in 1825, the same year that Standard Life was established, following in the footsteps of his grand-father and father who had also studied medicine there (although Erasmus, Charles' brother, was studying medicine at the time at Christ's in Cambridge[8]). Charles was not yet 17 when he entered the university.[9] The University of Edinburgh was a reasonable choice:

"Edinburgh [at the time] was better equipped, better staffed, and offered better hospital facilities than the cloistered English universities. It turned out not only better-educated MDs than Oxford and Cambridge, but vastly more of them. Edinburgh had long been a haven for wealthy Dissenters, barred from Oxford and Cambridge by the Thirty-nine Articles [that closed the two

---

[7] Cosh (2003), pp.65-6 and Herman (2002). pp.274-5.

[8] However, the family arranged for Erasmus to do one year of his required studies at the medical school in Edinburgh, so he was able to accompany his younger brother and they lived and studied together in the city. The fact that the Darwin family had for generations been staunch Whigs made Edinburgh – where Tory dominance and corruption was being challenged (which also negatively affected the quality of professors appointed with patronage to the university's medical school) – an attractive location for the boys. A graphic description of Charles Darwin's life in Edinburgh is to be found in Desmond, A. and Moore, J. 1991. *Darwin*. London: Penguin Books, chapters 2 and 3.

[9] The year that Charles entered, the University of Edinburgh's medical school enrolled 900 pupils, one-quarter of them from England.

universities to non-Anglicans[10]]. Here they studied a wide range of medical and scientific subjects, including botany, chemistry, and natural history. The students were also exposed to the latest Continental thought, particularly in the thriving extramural schools clustered around the university. Many graduates went to Paris after their final year and returned full of the latest French notions. They kept Edinburgh students briefed on the best, the most heterodox, and the most innovative new sciences...".[11]

However, apart from his interest in chemistry, Charles found his lectures "...intolerably dull". Materia Medica, taught by a Dr Duncan (a friend of Charles' father) at 8.00 in the morning during the winter term, Charles regarded as "...something fearful to remember" while the lectures on anatomy given by Professor Alexander Monro III were judged to be "...as dull as he was himself, and the subject disgusted me". But perhaps Charles' decisive experience at the medical school involved the witnessing, as he was required to do, of two operations performed without the aid of an anaesthetic. One was "...on a child, but I rushed away before they were complete". He never could be persuaded to attend another operation. As he later recalled, "...the two cases fairly haunted me for many a long year".[12] After two years Charles Darwin left Edinburgh for Cambridge from where HMS Beagle beckoned.

LINKING WITH OTHER INVESTMENT MANAGEMENT SPECIALISTS IN EDINBURGH

In 1881 a reduction in the rate of interest on heritable securities in Scotland provided the incentive for Standard Life to review its investment policy and look more seriously towards investment in riskier assets and more direct involvement in the growing industries. Over the succeeding few years the company made loans

---

[10] Herman (2002), p.275.
[11] Desmond, A. and Moore, J. (1991), p.22.
[12] Cosh (2003), pp.812-3.

to two English iron companies, to the Barrow Shipbuilding Co (owned by the Duke of Devonshire) and, in 1900, to an advanced Copenhagen-based company of shipbuilders and engineers. Standard Life also became more heavily involved in the finance of property development.

But it was the company's greater involvement in riskier assets that constituted a sea-change in its investment policy. In 1891 Standard Life obtained permission from its shareholders to change its investment regulations to allow for the purchase of debentures and preference shares in the UK and British dependencies, shortly thereafter adding the United States and other foreign territories. In 1896 a structural change took place in the company's long-term assets. Although over the previous decade debentures and preference shares averaged somewhat under 3% of total long-term assets, in 1896 the proportion leapt to 9.7%. In 1906 the percentage was 20.4% as shown in Exhibit 5.1. However, the proportion held in ordinary shares was negligible, amounting to 0.2% and 0.0% respectively in these two years.

Exhibit 5.1. Proportion of Standard Life's long-term assets held in the form of debentures and preference shares (£s)

Date	Percentage
1887	2.4
1896	9.7
1906	20.4

Source: Moss (2000), Appendix 6, p.386.

Significantly, however, the considerable increase in the weighting given to riskier assets in Standard Life's long-term assets was not accompanied by a proportional increase in the number of staff employed by the company to take care of its holdings. Rather, Standard Life turned to specialists both in Edinburgh and in London to provide the necessary expertise while closely monitoring the information and advice they provided. Particularly important providers of expertise were stock-brokers and the managers of investment trusts.

Stockbrokers and Investment Trusts

In Edinburgh Standard Life turned to the stockbrokers, Bell Cowan,[13] and to James Ivory, whose firm Ivory & Sime was an important manager of investment trusts. Indeed, in 1906 James Ivory became a director of Standard Life.[14] Robert Fleming, who was one of the early pioneers of the investment trust industry beginning his activities in the jute industry in Dundee and who at this time lived in London where he had established a merchant bank that bore his name, was employed as an equity adviser with particular responsibility for advising on American equity holdings. Other Edinburgh managers of investment trusts such as Martin Currie, which was originally solely an accounting firm, and stock-brokers that had stock to place made deals with Standard Life. Standard Life established similar links with London firms, in particular with the stockbrokers James Capel with whom the company had long had a relationship.[15]

In the late 1920s, Standard Life made a radical change in its asset allocation, increasing significantly the proportion of its equity holding. This is shown in Exhibit 5.2.

---

[13] Bell, Cowan & Co was founded by William Bell, an Edinburgh accountant, who formed a stockbroking firm under his name in 1845, the year after the Edinburgh Stock Exchange was established in December 1844. In 1858 Bell became chairman of the Edinburgh Stock Exchange. In 1879 Bell was joined by David Cowan, CA, and from 1887 to 1966 the firm was called Bell, Cowan & Co (William Bell having died in 1884). The firm is now known as Bell Lawrie White & Co Ltd. In 1989 it was acquired by TSB and in 1993 Brewin Dolphin Holdings acquired it from TSB. [Archer, A. et al. 2000. *The Making of Brewin Dolphin*. Newport News: Essex, pp.111-5.

[14] Moss (2000), p.170. Ivory was increasingly considered an expert on North America, where he had close ties with the New York firm of G.M. Forman & Co and in Chicago with Peabody, Houghteling & Co which was linked to J.P. Morgan.

[15] ibid, pp.117-20.

Exhibit 5.2. Standard Life's changing asset allocation, 1920-29 (%)

Date	Debenture and Preference Shares	Ordinary Shares	UK Mortgages	Property
1920	7.8	0.5	3.9	6.3
1925	23.9	1.7	2.1	3.5
1929	34.2	15.7	2.6	2.5

Source: Moss (2000), Appendix 6, p.386.

In fact, the shift in asset allocation was not simply in the direction of equities but rather to marketable securities more generally. Over this period, holdings of marketable securities (government stocks, debentures, preference shares and ordinary shares) increased from about 65% to about 85%, largely as a result of the increased holding of ordinary shares.[16] This shift reflected changing beliefs in Standard Life regarding the expected performance of the available alternative asset classes. Research done by some of the company's actuaries showed the superior long-term performance of equities. But the company was also influenced by the ideas of John Maynard Keynes who emphasised the importance of the flexibility that marketable securities provided, a belief that he was implementing as chairman of National Mutual.[17]

To begin with, Standard Life only purchased shares in investment trusts.[18] In the late 1920s, investment trusts themselves were switching more of their investments into equities. The British

---

[16] ibid, p.194.

[17] ibid, p.194. See Skidelsky, R. 1992. *John Maynard Keynes – The Economist as Saviour, 1920*-37. London, pp.25-6. In the *General Theory*, Keynes (1961) argued that stock markets are dominated by "...the fetish of liquidity", that is "...the doctrine that it is a positive virtue on the part of investment institutions to concentrate their resources upon the holding of 'liquid' securities" (p.155). By holding liquid assets an investor has the opportunity to "...switch investments to take advantage of short-term price movements which may be unrelated to long-term fundamentals". Moss (2000), p.260.

[18] ibid, p.194.

economy was growing rapidly at the time, inflation was increasing (undermining the returns on fixed-interest securities) and, after the introduction of the Corporation Profits Tax in 1921, ordinary and preference shares provided a source of income on which no additional corporation tax was payable. Between 1926 and 1929, 78 new investment trusts were established in the UK.[19] Through their large holdings of equities, investment trusts were able to spread risk, an attractive characteristic for Standard Life. However, as the company successfully accumulated its own competencies in collecting and analysing information on investment opportunities through the organisation of its internal investment function (see below), so its confidence grew to invest increasingly in individual companies. In some cases Standard Life became the largest single shareholder in several of the UK's best-known companies.

In 1926 the board of Standard Life approved a list of 55 stockbrokers that included some of the most famous London firms like Laing & Cruikshank, Messel & Co, Kitcat & Aitkin and Helbert Wagg & Co.[20] By 1950, some 25% of Standard Life's stock market transactions were being conducted through the London stock broking firm, Cazenove, while Bell Cowan of Edinburgh was next in order of importance.[21]

In the 1960s, following in the path of James Ivory who in 1906 became a director of Standard Life, Jimmy Gammell, a partner in Ivory & Sime, served as a member of the company's board.

In this way the expertise already available in Edinburgh greatly eased Standard Life's change in its asset allocation. From the point of view of the stockbrokers and specialist fund managers who provided their knowledge, Standard Life was a customer of growing importance. The changing needs of this customer as circumstances in the financial and investment markets shifted constituted an important source of learning for all concerned.

---

[19] Newlands (1997), p.175.
[20] Moss (2000), p.194.
[21] ibid, p.195.

ORGANISATION OF STANDARD LIFE'S INVESTMENT FUNCTION

In view of the knowledge already accumulated in stock broking firms and specialist investment managers (originally mainly the managers of investment trusts), both in Edinburgh and in London, it proved unnecessary for Standard Life to employ a large staff to gather information about investment opportunities. In fact, Standard Life had a tiny investment department. In 1925 the investment department employed only one investment manager, three clerks, and one typist. By 1950, this had grown to eight clerks and three typists, in addition to the investment manager, as is shown in Exhibit 5.3.[22] Clearly, by the mid-1920s a sophisticated division of labour had already occurred in London and Edinburgh regarding the acquisition, analysis and dissemination of knowledge concerning potentially profitable investments, not only in the UK but around the world. By 'plugging into' this division of labour, Standard Life was able rapidly to make a fundamental change in its asset allocation and give much higher priority to equities.

During the 1950s Standard Life was making new investments of between £15 and £30 million per annum. In 1961 the company's proportional holding of ordinary shares reached a peak of 43% of all assets. However, the directors of the company, through the investment committee continued to exercise tight control over the investment department. In part, this control was exercised through the mandate system whereby the investment committee mandated the investment department to make purchases of securities in limited instalments throughout the year. The problem was that while the mandate system gave the directors control, it prevented the investment department from taking advantage of Keynes' advice to use the liquidity of the company's securities in order to move quickly to benefit from new opportunities. According to Standard Life's official historian: "The directors appear to have had little confidence in the investment department being able to time such interventions correctly".[23]

---

[22] ibid, p.226.
[23] ibid, p.255.

Exhibit 5.3. Standard Life's internal organisation of the investment function

```
┌──────────────────────────────────────────────────────────┐
│   ┌────────────────────────────────────────────────┐     │
│   │                                                  │     │
│   │          INVESTMENT COMMITTEE                    │     │
│   │                                                  │     │
│   └────────────────────────────────────────────────┘     │
│                          │                                 │
│                          ▼                                 │
│   ┌────────────────────────────────────────────────┐     │
│   │                                                  │     │
│   │          INVESTMENT DEPARTMENT                   │     │
│   │   •  1925 employed 1 investment manager, 3 clerks│     │
│   │      and 1 typist.                               │     │
│   │   •  1950 employed 1 investment manager, 8 clerks│     │
│   │      and 3 typists.                              │     │
│   │   •  Function:  following the mandate of the     │     │
│   │      investment committee; buying/selling        │     │
│   │      securities; interacting with stockbrokers   │     │
│   │      and investment managers; monitoring the     │     │
│   │      performance of investments; collecting      │     │
│   │      information; preparing reports for the       │     │
│   │      investment committee.                       │     │
│   └────────────────────────────────────────────────┘     │
└──────────────────────────────────────────────────────────┘
```

Standard Life's investment department "…remained tiny compared with those of other life offices and only began to be strengthened after 1968", at a time when the UK stock market was performing well. However, it remained out of the question "…that Standard Life would try to emulate 'a successful "performance" mutual fund or a successful active investment trust' by regularly switching investments, even if this was what managed funds demanded".[24]

In 1972 a "…radical overhaul"[25] of the investment department was undertaken in an attempt to improve Standard Life's ability to manage pension funds. Staffing levels were increased and an economics research department was established, the head of which was sent for training to the Prudential.[26] However, the economics research department conflicted with the investment department which "…was more comfortable with the research and information received from stockbrokers"[27] and after several years the two departments were merged. In addition, greater emphasis was placed on research by investment staff.

In October 1972 the mandate system, which had proved cumbersome, was abandoned and the executive committee was given far greater freedom in deciding on the timing and quantity of purchases. The investment committee retained control only over sector distribution of investments. After the 'Big Bang' in 1986 the size of the investment committee was again increased substantially.

In 1994, further important changes were made to Standard Life's investment department. In this year Sandy Crombie took over from David Simpson as General Manager (Investment and Development). There were two major challenges that he faced. The first, according to Standard Life's official history, was the investment department's "…low profile within the company". The second was "…the need to respond to the ever-increasing competition from [outside specialist] fund managers".[28] To meet

---

[24] ibid, p.270.

[25] ibid, p.276.

[26] The Prudential's economics research department, established in 1958, at this time employed more macroeconomists than the Treasury.

[27] Moss (2000), p.276.

[28] ibid, p.330.

these challenges, Crombie instituted several changes that included the following:

- A 'house view' was created by bringing together all the forecasts for all international equity markets. This house view would drive stock selection and asset allocation. Senior investment managers from the client fund management team and the asset class management team would provide daily reviews. The first house view was produced in January 1995 and was welcomed as making an improved contribution.
- In order to give the investment department greater freedom to manage the company's main life fund, the many board resolutions with an impact on investment were combined into a single statement on group investment and lending policies.

One of Crombie's motivations in making these changes was to renew Standard Life's efforts in competing in the market for managed funds. However, according to the official history: "The response was disappointing". The reason was that "…prospective clients [questioned] whether 'a life company could ever be a premier investment manager'. Many believed that fund managers were much more committed to developing their capability, because they were dedicated to just one business…" and this favoured specialist fund managers when clients placed their mandates.[29]

As a result of this sentiment the gap between the external funds managed by specialist fund managers and those managed by insurance companies widened further. This is shown in Exhibit 5.4.

Exhibit 5.4 shows the amount of external funds managed by three financial institutions. [This figure serves as a measure of competitiveness in the market for managed funds – although it should be noted that the figure for Baillie Gifford is for 1997, one year later than those for the other two firms.] Prudential is the largest UK insurance company while Standard Life is the largest European mutual life insurance company. Baillie Gifford is Scotland's largest independent specialist investment management

---

[29] ibid, p.330.

company. Standard Life's lack of relative competitiveness was confirmed by the fact that in 1996 the company "…still had difficulty in recruiting staff in a very competitive market in which it was perceived to be more rewarding to work for fund managers".[30]

Exhibit 5.4. External funds managed, 1996-1997 (£ billions)

Financial Institution	External Funds Managed (£ bn)	Date
Baillie Gifford	£13	1997
Prudential	£10	1996
Standard Life	£2	1996

Source: Moss (2000), p.330; *CA Magazine*, December 1997, p.32 (for Baillie Gifford figure).

However, it was in 1998, during the global stock market boom, that the most radical change in the management of Standard Life's investment function took place. In January 1998, Scott Bell and Sandy Crombie decided to establish within the Standard Life group a wholly separate company to manage almost all of the group's assets and to market and sell a range of investment products and services on the external market for managed funds. This radical change in Standard Life's corporate organisation is shown in Exhibit 5.5.

---

[30] ibid, p.331.

Exhibit 5.5. Organisation of Standard Life Investments Limited, 16 November 1998

STANDARD LIFE GROUP

Standard Life Investments Ltd

Formed as a new company within the Standard Life Group, 16 November 1998

Standard Life Investments Limited was established on 16 November 1998. To emphasise its autonomy, the company moved in July 1999 to the old principal location of the Standard Life group at 3 George Street (that was re-designated as No.1 George Street). Collective investment, one of the effects of the equities boom, was increasingly being regarded as an alternative to both pensions and life assurance and it was hoped that the new status of Standard Life Investments Ltd would allow the company to compete more effectively in the market for managed funds. Legal & General, one of Standard Life's main competitors, had in 1997 overtaken Standard Life in terms of long-term assets, largely as a result of tracker funds it had established. This made Legal & General the second largest life insurance company after the Prudential. But at this time the Prudential, Legal & General and Standard Life all had long-term assets that exceeded those of

Norwich Union and Scottish Widows, the other major competitors.[31]

Standard Life Investments Ltd began by managing funds totalling £60 billion. The initial target was to double the company's share of the market for managed funds within five years. After the first year of operations the company's performance exceeded expectations with about £1.3 billion of new investment business being won, a significant proportion of which came from Canada where Standard Life had earlier established a separate investment company.[32]

In January 2004, however, just over five years since the creation of Standard Life Investments Ltd, the company was rocked by regulatory concerns over the solvency of the Standard Life group. These concerns followed both the stock market bust after March 2000 and the introduction of new regulations by the UK financial services regulator aimed at making more transparent the solvency of insurance companies. Figures released in December 2003 showed that Standard Life Investments had £87 billion of assets under management. This compared with £75 billion the previous year. According to the *Financial Times*: "Most industry observers agree that, while the firm failed to reach its ambitious five-year target of £100 billion, it has made steady progress in difficult market conditions. Indeed, one of the reasons for the launch of SLI was the group's plan to attract third-party funds, which now account for around a fifth of its assets, up from 9 percent five years ago".[33]

This allows a comparison to be made of Standard Life's external funds under management (i.e. from sources outside the company) with those of Baillie Gifford, Scotland's largest independent specialist investment manager. This comparison is shown in Exhibit 5.6.

As Exhibit 5.6 shows, while in 1996/7 Baillie Gifford's funds under management were about 6.5 times as large as Standard

---

[31] ibid, Figure 8.1, p.334. In the text (p.332) Moss states that it was in 1998 that Legal & General overtook Standard Life but Figure 8.1 shows this happening in 1997.

[32] ibid, p.334.

[33] *Financial Times*, January 18 2004.

Life's external managed funds, by 2003 they were about 1.3 times greater. Accordingly, although in the latter year Baillie Gifford, Scotland's largest independent specialist fund manager, was larger than Standard Life according to this measure, the gap had decreased since 1996/7.

Exhibit 5.6. Baillie Gifford and Standard Life's external funds under management, 1996-1997 and 2003 (£ billions)

Financial Institution	External Funds Managed, 1996/7 (£ bn)	External Funds Managed, 2003 (£ bn)	Ratio: BG/SL
Baillie Gifford	13.0	22.0	6.5 - 1996/7
			1.3 - 2003
Prudential	10.0	-	
Standard Life	2.0	17.4	

Source: Moss (2000), p.330; *CA Magazine*, December 1997, p.32 (for Baillie Gifford 1996/7 figure); implied from *Financial Times*, 18 January 2004 (for Standard Life 2003 figure); Scottish Financial Enterprise, 2003 Yearbook (for Baillie Gifford 2003 figure).

In confronting its 2004 crisis, one of the options that faced Standard Life was the possibility of de-mutualisation (discussed in the following section), a move that, according to the *Financial Times*: "...could lead to the flotation or sale of the fund management operation [i.e. SLI]".[34] However, in an interview with this newspaper, Sandy Crombie played down the prospect of a sale by emphasising the benefits to Standard Life of the in-house management of investment funds. He noted that the management fees on internally-managed assets tended to be lower than the average market rate. But the threat to Standard Life's mutual status was seen as a serious challenge, as is shown in the following section.

---

[34] *Financial Times*, 18 January 2004.

GOVERNANCE OF STANDARD LIFE

Standard Life's changing form of governance is shown in Exhibit 5.7. As can be seen, it was in 1925 that the company opted for mutualisation. As noted during Standard Life's 2004 crisis, the company had made a great deal of its mutual status in its core marketing message. This strongly emphasised the company's ability to take a long-term approach and the independence of its advice, both of these competitive advantages being attributed to its mutual status. According to Standard Life's online company profile: "The mutual status of our parent company makes us a rare breed among our peers. It allows us to focus solely on our clients and take a longer term view than some of our rivals". According to the *Financial Times*: "This mindset [regarding the benefits of mutualisation] has underpinned SLI's growing commitment to corporate governance. The firm, which owns 2 percent of the UK stock market, has been involved in most of the big shareholder revolts of the past decade".[35] The danger for Standard Life was that by losing its mutual status it would risk losing one of its main claims to distinctiveness.

Exibit 5.7. Standard Life's governance

Date	Form of Governance
1825	Partnership (shareholders personally liable for debts)
1910	Limited Company
1925	Mutualisation
2006	De-mutualisation

---

[35] ibid.

CONCLUSION

In July 2006, however, Standard Life abandoned its mutual status and listed on the London Stock Exchange. The circumstances under which this happened lie beyond the concerns of this book. Since then its shares have done well and the performance of SLI's investments is seen by other financial analysts as being relatively good. In the six months to the end of June 2007 Standard Life's profits before tax rose 73% compared to the same period in 2006. It is still too soon, however, to pronounce definitively on the costs and benefits of de-mutualisation to Standard Life and Standard Life Investments and their shareholders and customers.

CHAPTER

6

CONCLUSION

INTRODUCTION

Financial services and the oil and oil-related industry are the two most important industries in the Scottish economy in terms of contribution to Scottish GDP and employment as well as global competitiveness. Within the financial services industry the investment management sector is one of the most successful.

This book has largely been concerned with explaining why and how the Scottish, and in particular the Edinburgh, investment management sector achieved its prominence. In this concluding chapter a summary of the explanation is provided with the use of the key concepts of entrepreneurship and innovation, competencies and learning, organisation and globalisation.

ENTREPRENEURSHIP AND INNOVATION

In this book we have shown in some detail the significant initiating role played by entrepreneurs such as Robert Fleming, William Menzies, Carlyle Gifford and Sandy Crombie. Without the initiative taken by entrepreneurs such as these the investment management sector in Scotland and Edinburgh would not have taken off.

In large part, these entrepreneurs were initially involved in the provision of professional services – such as legal services in the case of Menzies and Gifford or accounting services in some of the other Scottish independent investment managers. In providing these services they came into contact with wealthy clients and also accumulated their own wealth. The next step was to help both their clients and themselves to invest some of this wealth in vehicles that would offer attractive rates of risk-adjusted return.

It was here, as shown in more detail in Chapter 1, that a key financial innovation entered the picture, the investment trust pioneered by Foreign & Colonial which was founded in 1868. This innovation was adopted by our entrepreneurs to achieve their investment purposes.

COMPETENCIES AND LEARNING

However, setting up an investment trust and raising the funds from appropriate pools of savings is one thing. Earning attractive rates of return – relative to other locally available rates – is quite another. The latter requires the accumulation of a set of complex and costly to acquire competencies. These competencies involve activities like gathering information about investment opportunities available, assessing the returns and risks involved in the investment, analysing the contextual opportunities and threats, etc. Bearing in mind that, as we have seen, the investments were often in far-flung places like the US, Asia, Australia and Latin America and that they were being made in the information and communication constrained 19th century, the magnitude of the task of successfully carrying out these activities can be appreciated.

In accumulating these competencies the learning process was obviously crucial. To some extent this required the entrepreneur to travel to the countries where the investments were located. For example, we saw that Robert Fleming made 64 visits to the United States while William Menzies made a total of 35. Learning also involved search, experimentation, experience, trial-and-error and reflection. These were not processes that anyone could master and there were, understandably, many failures.

However, perhaps the best indicator of successful learning and competence-building provided in this book is the success that Baillie Gifford achieved in both the US and Japan. In these export markets – markets for the export of investment management services – Baillie Gifford had to compete with the best, not only with US and Japanese financial firms but also with competitors from other parts of the world, including other UK competitors.

Baillie Gifford's success is proof of its *global* competitiveness (something we will return to later).

ORGANISATION

The Baillie Gifford example also illustrates the significance of organisation. In short, to be effective competencies must be appropriately organised. Take, for instance, equity investments. Here there are four units of analysis that have to be merged, each unit defining a frame around a set of specific issues: the firm (in which investment is being considered); the sector; the country; and the global context. But the need to deal with all these four units in constructing effective portfolios of equities raises difficult questions of organisation.

For example, should the firm have specialists in all four areas? How should knowledge be shared amongst the specialists? [For example, an analyst specialising in particular firms should also have knowledge of what is happening more generally in the sector to which those firms belong; and for some sectors – such as the information and communications sector – there are global dynamics that need to be understood.] Should teams of analysts be established according to countries or sectors or both and how should the global dimension be added? These kinds of questions give a taste of some of the organisational issues that must be resolved in carrying out the investment management function.

Once again, Baillie Gifford's success provides indirect evidence of the firm's ability to develop adequate solutions to these kinds of organisational problems (although this is not to say there is no room for further improvement).

GLOBALISATION

Finally, let us return to the issue of globalisation. My own study of the growth of firms in countries such as Japan, Korea, Taiwan and China points to the importance of learning and competence-accumulation through close involvement in the world's most dynamic markets. The same lesson is also to be learned from the experience of the investment management sector in Scotland and Edinburgh, as has been shown in detail in this book.

To begin with, in the late 19th and early 20th centuries, the investment trust managers were exporting funds they had acquired from local savings pools to the then-emerging countries – such as the US and Australia – which afforded higher rates of return. In the last quarter of the 20th century – as documented in the case of Baillie Gifford – it was fund management as a service that was exported. This service was sold, for example, to banks, pension funds and insurance companies in countries that included the US and Japan. Through close involvement in this service export market the 'Baillie Giffords' of Scotland and Edinburgh (including smaller investment management firms) have been able to learn from the best and improve their competencies further in much the same way that Sony, Samsung and Huawei have done. This export orientation is another element in the explanation of the success of investment management in Edinburgh, city of funds.

APPENDIX

EDINBURGH AS A PREMIER GLOBAL LOCATION FOR INVESTMENT MANAGEMENT

EDINBURGH'S IMPORTANCE

Edinburgh is one of the most important locations in Europe for investment management. Data on the leading European centres are given in Exhibit A.1.

Exhibit A.1. Europe's leading investment management centres, 2003

City	Funds under Management ($bn)
London	2,460.7
Paris	458.2
Zurich	413.6
Amsterdam	326.8
Frankfurt	310.9
Edinburgh*	205.0*
Milan	195.8

* The available statistics aggregate the funds managed in Edinburgh and Glasgow. The estimate of $205 billion for Edinburgh alone used here is based on the assumption that Edinburgh manages approximately 80% of the total for both cities of $252.7 billion. The figure of 80% is used since Edinburgh employs 80% of the total number of people employed in the fund management sector in both cities (see Exhibit A.10).

Source: 'Pan-European Perspectives: Financial Services International Benchmarking Report', Scottish Enterprise, 2003, p.50.

Edinburgh is also by far the smallest of the seven cities in terms of metropolitan population, as is shown in Exhibit A.2.

Exhibit A.2. Population of Europe's leading investment management centres, 2002

City	Metropolitan Population*	City Population
London	11,850,000	6,638,109
Paris	9,800,000	2,125,246
Milan	3,800,000	1,256,211
Amsterdam	2,100,000	735,080
Frankfurt	1,975,000	641,076
Zurich	1,188,00	337,000
Edinburgh	449,000	382,624

* Metropolitan areas include suburban areas.

FINANCIAL SERVICES[1] IN THE UK

By the end of the 1990s financial services made a more important contribution to the UK economy than manufacturing, contributing

---

[1]   At the two-digit primary SIC level, three financial services classifications are to be found: 65: financial intermediation except insurance and pension funding; 66: insurance and pension funding, except compulsory social security; and 67: activities auxiliary to financial intermediation. At five-digit level the following eight sub-sectors are to be found (with the total number of firms in each sub-sector given in brackets): banks (424); non-bank financial inter-mediation, i.e. non-banks, (1,240); trusts (4,777); life insurance (3,331); non-life insurance (476); activities auxiliary to financial intermediation (334); activities auxiliary to insurance (1,030); stock markets (616). (Pandit, Cook and Swann, 2001, p.41.)

a greater absolute amount to both GDP and employment. This is shown in Exhibit A.3.

Exhibit A.3. Contribution of financial services and manufacturing to UK GDP and employment (% of total), 1986 and 1998

	1986	**1998**
GDP		
Financial Services	21.7%	27.6%
Manufacturing	24.8%	19.7%
Employment		
Financial Services	13%	18.2%
Manufacturing	23%	17.1%

Source: CSO/ONS, UK National Accounts, 1990, 1999.

As Exhibit A.3 shows, while in 1986 manufacturing made a more important contribution both to UK GDP and employment, by 1998 this had changed. In 1998 the contribution of financial services was greater than that of manufacturing. In this year financial services was responsible for 27.6% of GDP compared to manufacturing's 19.7%. Financial services accounted for 18.2% of the UK's total employment while manufacturing was responsible for 17.1%.

THE CLUSTERING OF FINANCIAL SERVICES IN THE UK'S REGIONS

The financial services industry in the UK, like many other industries, is highly clustered, meaning that it is concentrated in geographical space. This is apparent from Exhibits A.4 and A.5 which show the geographical distribution of financial services activity in the UK by number of firms and employment respectively.

Exhibit A.4. Distribution of financial services firms by UK's top six regions (in terms of number of firms), 1997

Rank	Region	No. of Firms	Percentage
1	Greater London	5,430	55%
2	South East (Sussex & Surrey)	1,740	18%
3	North West (Greater Manchester)	843	9%
4	West Midlands (Hereford, Warwickshire, Staffordshire, etc)	666	7%
5	South West (Cornwall Devon, Dorset, Somerset etc)	640	7%
6	**South Scotland (mainly Edinburgh & Glasgow)**	**579**	**6%**

TOTAL: 9,898

Source: Calculated from Pandit, Cook and Swann (2001), p.43.

As can be seen from Exhibit A.4, South Scotland as a UK region is ranked sixth in the UK in terms of the number of financial services firms. It has 6% of the total number of financial services firms in the UK's top six regions or 579 firms out of a total of 9,898 firms in these six regions.

Scotland's employment in financial services is shown in Exhibit A.5 relative to the UK's other two main regions of employment in this industry, namely Greater London (mainly the City and Canary Wharf) and the South-West (mainly the Bristol area). While Scotland employs 10% of the total number of employees in the UK financial services industry, Greater London employs 32% and the South-West 7%.

Exhibit A.5. Distribution of financial services employment by UK's top three regions (in terms of employment), 1997

Employment	Region	Percentage
UK Total	*1,060,000*	*100%*
Greater London (mainly City & Canary Wharf)	340,000	32%
Scotland (mainly Edinburgh & Glasgow)	**111,000**	**10%**
South-West (mainly Bristol)	76,000	7%

Source: Pandit and Cook (2003), p.238.

THE FINANCIAL SERVICES INDUSTRY IN SCOTLAND

Contribution of the Financial Services Industry to the Scottish Economy

The contribution of the financial services industry to the Scottish economy is shown in Exhibit A.6.

Exhibit A.6. Estimated contribution of the Scottish financial services industry to the Scottish economy, 2003

Contribution	Percentage
Contribution to Scotland's GDP	7%*
Direct contribution to Scotland's employment	5%

* The contribution of the electronics industry was similar.
Source: Fraser of Allander Institute (2003).

As Exhibit A.6 shows, the financial services industry contributed an estimated 7% to the GDP of Scotland and made a direct contribution of 5% to total employment in Scotland. [Including indirect employment effects, the latter figure increases to about 10%.[2]]

Size and Composition of the Financial Services Industry in Scotland

How large is the financial services industry in Scotland? What are its most important sub-sectors?

Unfortunately, the statistical data that would provide a definitive answer to these questions do not exist. The best we have to go on is a study commissioned by Scottish Financial Enterprise (a private sector association representing Scottish financial firms) and Scottish Enterprise (the main Scottish government body with responsibility for encouraging economic development in Scotland) from the Fraser of Allander Institute at the University of Strathclyde.[3] The aim of the study was "...to assess the total

---

[2] Fraser of Allander Institute, University of Strathclyde, 'Economic Impact of Financial Services Sector on the Scottish Economy', 2003. Foreword by Professor Brian Ashcroft, p.3.
[3] Fraser of Allander Institute, University of Strathclyde, 'Economic Impact of Financial Services Sector on the Scottish Economy', 2003 (mimeo).

economic benefits that financial services provide to the Scottish economy".[4]

This study, published in 2003, defined the 'financial services industry' in terms of the membership of Scottish Financial Enterprise. Since not all financial firms in Scotland are members of Scottish Financial Enterprise, this has resulted in an under-estimation of the total employment in this industry. According to the Fraser of Allander study, total employment in the financial services industry in Scotland in 2003 amounted to 59,363. However, the official government figure for 1999 was 80,000.[5] As was shown in Exhibit A.5, drawing on Pandit and Cook (2003) that also used official UK government figures for 1997, the figure was 111,000.

Despite these difficulties, however, the Fraser of Allander study does seem to have reasonable estimates for the banking, life insurance, and fund management sub-sectors since these are relatively well-represented amongst the Scottish Financial Enterprise membership.[6] Since these are the three major sub-sectors in this industry in Scotland, the study is used here to present a description of the Scottish financial services industry. The main components of this industry are shown in Exhibit A.7.

As Exhibit A.7 clearly shows, banking, life assurance and insurance, and fund management and investment trusts are the three most important sub-sectors in the financial services industry in Scotland in terms of employment (that may also be taken as a proxy for value added for GDP purposes). In 2003, the study suggests, direct employment in these three sub-sectors was 25,542 in banking, 19,446 in life assurance and insurance, and 3,305 in fund management and investment trusts.[7]

---

[4]   ibid, p.3.

[5]   ibid. p.8.

[6]   This is less so in the case of building societies – the study included only two building societies, the Scottish Building Society and the Dunfermline, that together employed only 358 people, ibid, p.33.

[7]   Obviously, the three sub-sectors also generated additional indirect employment as employment in supplying sectors was stimulated and as a result of more general employment-multiplier effects.

Exhibit A.7. Employment in the financial services sector in Scotland[1]

Financial Firms	Total Employment	%
Banks	25,542	43.0
Life Assurance and Insurance	19,446	32.8
Fund Managers and Investment Trusts	**3,305**	**5.6**
Investment Administration[2]	2,600	4.4
Merchant Banks, Finance Companies and Corporate Advisers	1,149	1.9
Market Makers, Brokers, Dealers and Stockbrokers	459	0.8
Building Societies	361	0.6
Supporting Firms and Institutions		
Corporate Lawyers	3,477	5.9
Accountants and Tax Advisers	2,577	4.3
Actuaries and Insurance Advisers	300	0.5
Professional Institutions	146	0.2
Total	**59,363**	**100**

[1] The 'financial services sector' was defined for the purposes of this study in terms of the membership of Scottish Financial Enterprise (SFE). It is important to note that this has meant that there are some anomalies between the present data and other government data on the financial services sector in Scotland. Specifically, the estimate of total employment of 59,363 represents a significant underestimate. The government Labour Force Survey of 1999 estimated that there were 80,488 full-time equivalent employees employed in the Scottish financial services sector. Employment in building societies is also considerably understated since only two of the smaller building societies in Scotland were included.

[2] 'Investment Administration' refers to "…externally owned operators, who are largely involved in back-office processing operations" (Fraser of Allander Institute, 2003, p.5).

Source: Calculated from Fraser of Allander Institute, University of Strathclyde, 'Economic Impact of Financial Services Sector on the Scottish Economy', 2003.

Further information comparing the size and composition of the fund management sub-sectors in London and Scotland is given in Exhibit A.8. This information comes from the survey published in February 2001 by the Fund Managers' Association[8].

Exhibit A.8. Fund management in London and Scotland: assets under management and UK staff

Location	Firms (No.)	Assets under Management £bn (%)	UK Staff No. (%)	Investment Managers No. (%)
London	55.5*	1,715.0 (84.9)	18,014 (81.0)	3,027.5 (81.5)
Scotland	11.5*	291.6 (14.4)	3,474 (15.6)	652.5 (17.6)
Other	2	13.3 (0.7)	748 (3.4)	35 (0.9)
Total	**69**	**2,019.9 (100)**	**22,236 (100)**	**3,715 (100)**

* Figures for one firm with two main investment management offices – in London and in Scotland – have been divided evenly between the two centres.

Note: This data is based on a survey questionnaire completed by 69 of the FMA's 76 members, accounting for 94% of the assets managed by the latter members. The funds managed by the 76 members and their international associates totalled £7,000 billion of which £2,100 billion was managed in the UK.

Source: Fund Managers' Association Survey, February 2001.

---

[8]   The Fund Managers' Association at the time had 76 members of whom 69, or 91%, replied to the survey questionnaire. According to the FMA: "The firms replying probably account for 94 percent of the total assets managed by members". Fund Managers' Association, 'Fund Management Survey 2000', February, 2001, p.1. "The funds managed globally by our members and their international associates are £7,000 billion of which £2,100 billion is managed in the UK" (Foreword).

As implied in Exhibit A.8, London had 5.0 times as many fund management firms as Scotland, 5.9 times the amount of assets under management, 5.2 times as many staff, and 4.6 times as many investment managers. The average size of firm in London in terms of assets under management was £30.9 billion per firm, in terms of UK staff was 324.6 employees per firm and in terms of investment managers was 54.6 managers per firm. The corresponding figures for Scottish firms were: in terms of assets under management, £25.4 billion per firm; in terms of UK staff, 302.1 UK employees per firm; and in terms of investment managers, 56.7 managers per firm. This is shown in Exhibit A.9.

Exhibit A.9. Average size of fund management firms in London and Scotland

Location	Assets under Management (£bn per firm)	UK Employees (per firm)	Investment Managers (per firm)
London	£30.9	324.6	54.6
Scotland	£25.4	302.1	56.7

Source: Calculated from Exhibit A.8.

As Exhibit A.9 shows, Scottish fund management firms tended to be somewhat smaller on average in terms of both funds under management and UK employment. However, they were more 'investment manager-intensive', employing on average 56.7 investment managers compared to London's 54.6. Exhibit A.9 implies that while the London figure for assets under management per employee was £95.2 million per employee, the Scottish figure was £84.1 million per employee. The exhibit implies that Scottish firms are also more 'investment manager-intensive' than their London counterparts, with each Scottish investment manager on average managing £450 million of funds while London investment managers manage £570 million. Further research is needed, however, to answer whether the higher investment manager-intensity of Scottish firms is reflected in better performance.

CLUSTERING OF THE FUND MANAGERS AND INVESTMENT TRUSTS SUB-SECTOR WITHIN SCOTLAND

Within Scotland, the fund managers and investment trusts sub-sector is highly clustered with most activity in Edinburgh. According to the Fraser of Allander Institute study, there were a total of 19 firms in this sub-sector. Of these, ten are headquartered in Edinburgh. Only one Scottish-based firm (Murray Johnstone) and one substantial externally-owned firm (Britannic Asset Management) were located in Glasgow. One firm was headquartered in Aberdeen (Aberdeen Asset Management), while Dundee had one firm with headquarters in the city (Alliance Trust) and one branch of an Edinburgh-based firm (Edinburgh Fund Managers, i.e. the former Dunedin).[9] This implies that seven of the 19 firms, while undertaking fund management activities in Scotland, were headquartered outside Scotland. Most of these firms were located in Edinburgh.

Employment in the fund managers and investment trusts sub-sector in each of these cities is shown in Exhibit A.10.

---

[9]   Fraser of Allander Institute (2003), p.25. Edinburgh Fund Managers has since been taken over by Aberdeen Asset Management.

Exhibit A.10. Regional employment in the fund managers and investment trusts sub-sector in Scotland, 2003*

Region (LEC area)	Employment	Percentage
Lothian & Edinburgh Enterprise (Edinburgh)	**1,934**	**69.5**
Glasgow Development Agency (Glasgow)	464	16.7
Grampian Enterprise (Aberdeen)	254	9.1
Enterprise Tayside (Dundee)	129	4.6
Total	**2,783**	**100**

* Note that 'employment' refers only to those included in completed questionnaires.
Source: Fraser of Allander Institute (2003), p.25.

As shown in Exhibit A.10, 70% of the employment in the fund managers and investment trusts sub-sector is located in Edinburgh. Of the remaining three Scottish cities, 17% is in Glasgow, 9% in Aberdeen and 5% in Dundee. This makes Edinburgh the clearly dominant city in terms of fund management activity, a feature that has remained constant since the beginning of this sub-sector in the late 19th century.

BIBLIOGRAPHY

Ackrill, M. and Hannah, L. 2002. *Barclays.The Business of Banking 1690-1996*. Cambridge: Cambridge University Press.

Anderson, R.D., Lynch, M. and Phillipson, N. 2003. *The University of Edinburgh: An illustrated history*. Edinburgh: Edinburgh University Press.

Archer, A. et al. 2000. *The Making of Brewin Dolphin*. Newport News: Essex.

Brown, R. (ed). 2003. *A History of Accounting and Accountants*. Washington, DC: Beard Books.

Buchan, J. 2003. *Capital of the Mind: How Edinburgh changed the world*. London: John Murray.

Burton, H. and Corner, D.L. 1968. *Investment Trusts and Unit Trusts in Britain and America*. London.

Cameron, A. 1995. *Bank of Scotland, 1695-1995*. Edinburgh: Mainstream Publishing.

Cassis, Y. 1990. *Capitalism in a Mature Economy*. Aldershot: Edward Elgar.

Checkland, S.G. 1975. *Scottish Banking: A history, 1695-1973*. Glasgow: Collins.

Cobham, D. (ed). 1995. *Markets and Dealers: The economics of the London financial markets*. Harlow: Longman.

Collins, M. and Baker, M. 2003. *Commercial Banks and Industrial Finance in England and Wales, 1860-1913*. Oxford: Oxford University Press.

Cosh, M. 2003. *Edinburgh: The golden age*. Edinburgh: John Donald.

Cummings, A.J.G. and Devine, T.M. 1994. *Industry, Business and Society in Scotland since 1700: Essays presented to Professor John Butt*. Edinburgh: John Donald.

Davidson, A.R. 1956. *The History of the Faculty of Actuaries in Scotland, 1856-1956*. Glasgow: William Hodge.

Denholm, J.M. 1981. *One Hundred Years of Scottish Life: A history of the Scottish Life Assurance Company, 1881-1981.* Edinburgh: Chambers.

Dennett, L. 1998. *A Sense of Security: 150 years of Prudential.* Cambridge: Granta.

Desmond, A. and Moore, J. 1991. *Darwin.* London: Penguin Books.

Devine, T.M. 1999. *The Scottish Nation, 1700-2000.* London: Penguin.

— 2003. *Scotland's Empire, 1600-1815.* London: Allen Lane.

Fransman, M. 1995. *Japan's Computer and Communications Industry: The evolution of industrial giants and global competitiveness.* Oxford: Oxford University Press

— 1999. *Visions of Innovation: The firm and Japan.* Oxford: Oxford University Press.

— 2002. *Telecoms in the Internet Age: From boom to bust to...?.* Oxford: Oxford University Press. (Winner of the 2003 Wadsworth   Prize.)

— 2004. 'The Telecoms Boom and Bust 1996-2003 and the Role of Financial Markets'. *Journal of Evolutionary Economics,* 14(4): 369-406.

— (ed). 2006. *Global Broadband Battles: Why the US and Europe lag while Asia leads.* Palo Alto: Stanford University Press.

Fraser of Allander Institute, University of Strathclyde. 2003. 'Economic Impact of Financial Services Sector on the Scottish Economy'.   Mimeo.

Freeman, C. and Lõuça, F. 2002. *As Time Goes By: From the industrial revolutions to the information revolution.* Oxford: Oxford University Press.

Gifford, T.J.C. 1969. *Letters from America.* Edinburgh: T. & A. Constable.

Glasgow, G. 1932. *The Scottish Investment Trust Companies.* London.

Golding, T. 2003. *The City: inside the great expectation machine. Myth and reality in institutional investment and the stock market.* Harlow: Prentice Hall.

Greenwald, B. and Stiglitz, J.E. 1992. 'Information, Finance and Markets: The architecture of allocative mechanisms'. In V. Zamagni (ed), *Finance and the Enterprise*. London: Academic Press.

Herman, A. 2002. *The Scottish Enlightenment: The Scots' invention of the modern world*. London: Fourth Estate.

Hirschmann, A.O. 1970. *Exit, Voice and Loyalty: Responses to decline in firms, organizations and states*. Cambridge, Mass: Harvard University Press.

Jackson, W.T. 1968. *The Enterprising Scot: Investors in the American West after 1873*. Edinburgh:

Keynes, J.M. 1961. *General Theory of Employment, Interest and Money*. New York: Harcourt Brace and Co.

Kindleberger, C.P. 2000. *Manias, Panics and Crashes: A history of financial crises*. Basingstoke, Hampshire: Palgrave.

Klepper, S. 1997. 'Industry Life Cycles'. *Industrial and Corporate Change*, 6: 145-183.

Kynaston, D. 1994. *The City of London. Volume 1, A World of Its Own, 1815-1890*. London: Random House.

— 1995. *The City of London. Volume 2, Golden Years, 1890-1914*. London: Random House.

Lewin, C.G. 2003. *Pensions and Insurance Before 1800: A social history*. East Linton, Scotland: Tuckwell.

Michie, R.C. 1981. *Money, Mania and Markets: Investment, company formation and the stock exchange in nineteenth-century Scotland*. Edinburgh: John Donald.

Moss, M. 2000. *Standard Life, 1825-2000: The building of Europe's largest mutual life company*. Edinburgh: Mainstream Publishing.

Munn, C.W. 1994. 'The Emergence of Edinburgh as a Financial Centre'. In A.J.G. Cummings and T.M. Devine (eds), *Industry, Business and Society in Scotland since 1700: Essays presented to Professor John Butt*. Edinburgh: John Donald.

Nairn, A. 2002. *Engines That Move Markets. Technology investing from railroads to the Internet and beyond*. New York: John Wiley.

Newlands, J. 1997. *Put Not Your Trust in Money: A history of the investment trust industry from 1868 to the present day*. London: Chappin Kavanagh.

North, D. 1990. *Institutions, Institutional Change and Economic Performance.* Cambridge: Cambridge University Press.

Pandit, N.R. and Cook, G.A.S. 2003. 'The benefits of industrial clustering: Insights from the British financial services industry at three locations'. *Journal of Financial Services Marketing,* 7(3): 230-245.

— and Swann, G.M.P. 2001. 'The Dynamics of Industrial Clustering in British Financial Services'. *The Service Industries Journal,* 21(4): 33-61.

Perez, C. 2002. *Technological Revolutions and Financial Capital.* Cheltenham: Edward Elgar.

The Royal Bank of Scotland. Undated. *The Royal Bank of Scotland, 1727-1977.* Edinburgh: The Royal Bank of Scotland.

Saville, R. 1996. *Bank of Scotland: A history, 1695-1995.* Edinburgh: Edinburgh University Press.

Schumpeter, J.A. 1934. *The Theory of Economic Development.* Department of Economics: Harvard University.

— 1939. *Business Cycles: A Theoretical, Historical and Statistical Analysis of the Capitalist Process.* New York: McGraw-Hill, 2 vols.

— 1966. *Capitalism, Socialism and Democracy.* London: Unwin.

Scottish Biographies. 1938. Glasgow: Jackson, Son & Co.

Scottish Enterprise. 2003. 'Pan-European Perspectives: Financial Services International Benchmarking Report'. Glasgow: Scottish Enterprise.

Skidelsky, R. 1992. *John Maynard Keynes – The Economist as Saviour, 1920-37.* London: Macmillan.

Slaven, A. and Checkland, S. (eds). 1990. *Dictionary of Scottish Business Biography, Vol. 2: Processing, Distribution, Services.* Aberdeen: Aberdeen University Press.

Smith, B. 2000. *Robert Fleming, 1845-1933.* Haddington, Scotland: Whittinghame House.

Smout, T.C. 1969. *A History of the Scottish People, 1560-1830.* Glasgow: William Collins.

Souden, D. 2003. *The Bank and the Sea: The Royal Bank of Scotland Group and the finance of shipping since 1753.* Edinburgh: The Royal Bank of Scotland Group.

Stiglitz, J. 2003. *The Roaring Nineties: Seeds of destruction.* London: Allen Lane.

Van Helten, J.J. and Cassis, Y. (eds). 1990. *Capitalism in a Mature Economy: Financial institutions, capital exports and British industry, 1870-1939.* Aldershot: Edward Elgar.

Weir, R.B. 1973. *A History of the Scottish American Investment Company Limited 1873-1973.* Edinburgh.

Printed in the United Kingdom
by Lightning Source UK Ltd.
125720UK00002B/76-93/A